AL MARCHESE
EMILIO PUCCI
DI BARSENTO
LA CRITICA DI
MODA ITALIANA

ARMANDO CHITOLINA (Ed.)

LAUDOMIA PUCCI
VANESSA FRIEDMAN
ALESSANDRA AREZZI BOZA
DYLAN COLUSSI

Emilio

Pucci Fashion Story

TASCHEN

Contents

Foreword

Laudomia Pucci

It is an Italian tradition for children to join the family business, be it car manufacturing or fashion, and although I hadn't trained as a designer—I studied politics at university—when the time came, just before graduation, I found myself gobbled up "Italian style," and working at my father's side. In the 35 years since then, I have been busy carrying forward the vision my father left. Thanks to his teachings, as well as to the valuable help from LVMH and Bernard Arnault himself, not to mention all the talented and dedicated people who have worked by my side, we have been able to bring the Pucci brand into the 21st century and recreate its magic across continents.

That magic is rooted in my father's uncompromising—and unprecedented—view of elegance, femininity, and chic. He was a minimalist before minimalism; a jet-setter before jets were flying; a scientist before fabric technology became a discipline; provocative in his modernity and sartorial daring. For him, prints were rhythm and movement, and in prints he expressed a message of contagious happiness. He enjoyed beauty in every form: laughter, nature, and youth!

The melting pot that created this singular sensibility was the product of Neapolitan grandeur, courtesy of his mother, and Russian extravagance, thanks to his father, who was three-quarters Russian. It's a piece of "the Italian dream, of living like the Italians" that turned the words "Made in Italy" into a synonym of excellence and quality.

Brought together in one aesthetic, these elements never fail to produce emotion in people when they see the products. Many a time I have heard a woman say: "When I met my husband I was wearing Pucci"; or, "When I left my husband I was wearing my favorite Pucci," and this happened over decades. As Martha Duffy wrote in *Time* magazine in May 1990, "Life must be sweet to Emilio Pucci. There can be few satisfactions more pleasing to a designer than to savor success twice, to lead fashion's promenade after years on the shelf. A quarter-century ago, Pucci introduced bodysuits in vivid geometric patterns..."

It's a generational story that is continuing to evolve as the Millennials and Generation Z discover Pucci for themselves—and not just them. Through the years I've been called to paint a plane in "Pucci" print and cover a pool in Pucci's inspired Bisazza mosaic, to celebrate the heritage's creativity with mannequins and to collaborate with artists. But most of all I've been told a Pucci piece is forever, be it just a scarf!

TEL. 055 / 283061 - 62
TELEX 571171 PUCCI T
FAX. 055 - 28 04 51
COD. FISC.
PART. IVA 00395510480

CASA DI ALTA MODA
"EMILIO PUCCI S.R.L."
PALAZZO PUCCI
6, VIA DE' PUCCI
50122 FIRENZE - ITALIA

TELEFAX TRANSMISSION

To the attention of: D.ssa Laudomia Pucci
From : Emilio Pucci fax 55-280451
Date : 25th February 1991

This transmission consists of 2 pages.

Please telephone, telex or telefax our office in the event of an error in transmission.

Dear Lao,

Here is the shortest article I could write concerning the Award should you have to talk to the press, or there, or should someone else wish to know my views.

Best luck,

Love Emilio

Please take note of new fax number - 55/280451.

1936: REED COLLEGE, PORTLAND, OREGON. AN ITALIAN STUDENT NAMED EMILIO PUCCI, WHO HAPPENS TO BE THE CAPTAIN AND INSTRUCTOR OF THE COLLEGE SKI TEAM, DESIGNS THE UNIFORM FOR THE TEAM. THE UNIFORM IS MADE BY A SMALL LOCAL FIRM CALLED WHITE STAG.

1948: THE CHRISTMAS ISSUE OF HARPER'S BAZAAR SHOWS PICTURES OF PUCCI SKIWEAR SOLD AT LORD & TAYLOR'S. THE HEADING OF THE STORY IS: " AN ITALIAN SKIER DESIGNS". WHITE STAG, BY NOW AN OUTSTANDING SKIWEAR MANUFACTURER, PRODUCES UNDER THE EMILIO PUCCI LABEL A COLLECTION WHICH IS SOLD AT LORD & TAYLOR'S.

1954: DALLAS, TEXAS. PUCCI RECEIVES FROM STANLEY MARCUS THE NEIMAN MARCUS AWARD FOR DISTINGUISHED SERVICE IN THE FIELD OF FASHION.

25TH FEBRUARY 1991: NEW YORK. PUCCI IS AWARDED THE C.F.D.A.

55 YEARS HAVE ELAPSED SINCE PUCCI, THE REED COLLEGE STUDENT, SKETCHED HIS FIRST DESIGN. OVER HALF A CENTURY HAS ELAPSED. ON THIS DAY PUCCI WOULD LIKE TO DEDICATE THIS AWARD TO THE CITY OF FLORENCE, FROM WHERE, AFTER THE DARK MEDIAEVAL AGES, THE GREAT MESSAGE OF RENAISSANCE WENT OUT TO THE WORLD WITH ITS UNIVERSAL RELIGIOUS SIGNIFICANCE, AND THE MIRACLE OF ART, CREATIVITY, BEAUTY AND HARMONY. A MESSAGE OF HOPE AND PROMISE FOR ALL HUMANITY DURING ONE OF THE MOST SERIOUS MOMENTS IN HISTORY.

Page 1: Drawing for "Emilio of Capri" logo, 1950. China ink on tracing paper, 19 x 20 cm.

Page 2: Portrait of Emilio Pucci, Marchese di Barsento by Brunetta. The portrait is dedicated and signed by the foremost Italian fashion journalists and editors-in-chief on the occasion of the Premio Critica della Moda Italiana, 1960s.

Page 4: Emilio Pucci on the terrace of Villa Settanni in Capri, 1950.

Page 6: Laudomia Pucci in the "Sala Bianca" Ballroom in the offices at Palazzo Pucci, Florence 1990.
Photo: Torrini.

Pages 8–9: Letter from Emilio Pucci to his daughter Laudomia on the eve of her accepting the CFDA Award on his behalf, in which he sums up the milestones of his career, 1991.
Courtesy Emilio Pucci Archive, Florence.

Below left: Drawing given by Emilio Pucci to his daughter Laudomia for her seventh birthday; the letters of her name are decorated with flowers.

Right: Laudomia Pucci at the age of nine in the garden of the Villa di Granaiolo, the family estate.

Opposite: Emilio and Laudomia Pucci in Palazzo Pucci, Florence, 1986.

Aristocratic Design

Vanessa Friedman

Once upon a time, in the waning years of the first decade of the 21st century, a party was held in a grand 15th-century palazzo in Florence, a stone's throw from the Duomo in the heart of the city. Guests came from England, from the United States, from Australia; they came from the North of Italy and the South, from France and Greece and Russia. There were sixty-somethings, there were twenty-somethings; the women were wearing long dresses and short, fur jackets, the men tuxedos; and as they stood in the elegant courtyard of the grand stone building, amid marble busts and behind ornate wrought-iron gates, nibbling canapés and laughing, a host of enormous helium-filled balloons in a swirling rainbow of colors and designs rose above their heads like gigantic champagne bubbles, floating toward the sky.
"It was," says the communications mogul Karla Otto, who helped organize the event, "a magic night."
It was a night when the pop superstar Kylie Minogue, in psychedelic sequined mini dress, met the French businesswoman Delphine Arnault in floor-sweeping rainbow silk; when actress/swimsuit designer Elizabeth Hurley in corseted kaleidoscopic chiffon met Italian aristocrat Georgiana Corsini; when French blue blood Arielle de Rothschild met the American ambassador to Rome, Ronald Spogli, who met the young British designer Matthew Williamson. It was a night when the past melded seamlessly into the present and the present snuggled up to the future, and they all relaxed together and had a drink. There was, says Karla Otto, almost no one who was invited to the party who didn't want to come. Which is fairly extraordinary, given the nominal reason for the event: celebrating the 60th anniversary of a fashion brand.
After all, by the end of the 20th century, celebrating the anniversaries of fashion brands had become something of a trend, and the

fashion world, from media to consumers, had in turn become a little jaded. But then, the fashion brand in question was not just any fashion brand. It was Emilio Pucci. And Emilio Pucci has always been, and still is today, about much more than clothes.

It is about, first of all, a man: Emilio Pucci, Marchese di Barsento, an extraordinary, charismatic figure—a sportsman, adventurer, tastemaker, entrepreneur—with a singular appetite for life. He had the vision to see beyond social norms to a future of freedom, and then apply that vision to the creation of clothing, starting in 1949 with a jewel box of a shop on the island of Capri, holiday resort of the rich and famous.

It is about a family: the Puccis, a name so embedded in the history of Florentine nobility they not only have the palazzo to show for it but also a street, the Via dei' Pucci, and an ancestry that can be traced back to both Lorenzo de Medici and Catherine the Great.

It is about an ancestral home: the Renaissance palazzo built by the Puccis, which has fallen into decline and risen again (and done so more than once), which is filled with frescoes and busts and filigree, and whose walls have sheltered past generations and will shelter generations to come. The palazzo provided Emilio with a never-ending source of inspiration, and became the seat of the business.

It is about evolution: how a family company that started with a bijou store on a resort island ended up with a majority ownership by Moët Hennessy-Louis Vuitton, the largest luxury group in the world; how a brand named after a single person was able to live on beyond that person, and thrive in the hands of a number of other designers without ever losing its central identity.

Page 12: 60th anniversary of the Pucci Company, 2007: an installation by Gerard Cholot in the courtyard of Palazzo Pucci.
Photo: Alessandro Ciampi.

Opposite: 60th anniversary of the Pucci Company, 2007: "The Colored Rooms," an installation by Maria Luisa Frisa, inspired by the historical boutique in Palazzo Pucci.
Photo: Alessandro Ciampi.

"Palio di Siena" scarf, 1960s.
Silk twill, 90 x 90 cm.

Opposite: Printed silk crêpe scarf dress featuring the "Ottagoni" motif, embroidered all over with Swarovski crystals. Fall/Winter 1967 Collection. Photo: Lumachi, Florence.

Fashion show for the Spring/Summer 1966 Collection in Palm Springs. Photo: William K. Plachta.

And it is about innovation: Pucci was not only the first real Italian ready-to-wear brand, but also one of the first to bear a logo, to diversify into other design areas such as interiors and sports wear, to exploit technology, and to create fabrics that could be tossed into a handbag for ease of travel.

But above all, it is about an idea, which had something to do with how women dressed, and something to do with how the world worked, but mostly had to do with women themselves.

What was it? "Freedom and seduction," said Stephan Janson, who worked as a designer for Pucci in 1998, after the founder had passed away.

"Modernity and style and happiness," says Carla Sozzani, owner of the internationally influential Milanese boutique 10 Corso Como and ex-editor of Italian *Elle*.

"As clothing, it accepted your style of life, and didn't try to transform it," says Clarice Pecori Giraldi, former managing director of Christie's, Italy, who grew up in Florence with the Pucci family.

It was both specific, composed of certain immutable values (ease, color, lifestyle references), and general enough (engaged with the liberty of the body and soul) to evolve over time. Consider the fact that author and American blue blood Marina Rust remembers her grandmother wearing Pucci for dinners at home, and decades later she herself wears Pucci for dinners at home. Indeed, the remarkable thing about Pucci is that the stories the women tell about the brand are so similar, no matter where the women live and no matter what age they are. Pucci is ever-present in their quotidian life just as much as it is in their memories of the past.

For example, Karla Otto, a German based in London, says: "I have always had a real attraction for Pucci, and I use that word literally—there's something reflexive and

Pages 18/19: Emilio Pucci drawing in his studio in Palazzo Pucci, 1959. Photo © David Lees/Corbis Historical/ Getty Images.

Fashion show for the Spring/Summer 1969/70 Collection in Honolulu, Hawaii. Photo: Mike Janis for Foto Impressions.

Opposite: Detail of the drawing for "Tulipani" panel, 1965. Colored pencil on paper, 190 x 130 cm.

unconscious about how it makes me feel happy; it's uplifting and makes me feel very feminine. After a long day, you go home, take a shower, put on a Pucci dress, go out, and feel great. You shine. Almost always, people comment."

According to Pecori Giraldi: "It's one of those things I'll put on in the morning if I need a boost, or if I need to feel at ease. I have a turquoise-blue dress, for example, that I wore to the opening of Christie's in Italy, and I have a photo of me and Gio Moretti standing at the top of the stairs to greet people, and I am all Pucci, Pucci, Pucci—but I also wore this dress on my honeymoon in the Hamptons." And ex–American *Vogue* fashion editor Polly Mellen, from New York, says: "When I went on my honeymoon in 1952, we went to Capri, and I said to my husband Louis, 'I have to have a Pucci,' and we went to the little shop down a cobblestone street that was just filled with color, and I got an outfit—I've never had a pair of pants that fit like that. A pair of those pants, and a silk shirt that weighed nothing with a bateau neckline, and, my God, you felt you looked better than everyone else in the room, except everyone else in the room was wearing the same thing! Later, when I got remarried, I wore my Puccis again, when we would go to the Cedarhurst hunt club."

This is the difference between a fashion company that is designer-led and associated with a specific silhouette or way of cutting that situates it firmly in a place and time, such as Dior's New Look, or Courrèges' space-age minis, and a fashion company whose ethos is less about aesthetic purity than an emotional and social idea: one that can be reinterpreted and refined as necessary, and that can be seen through multiple imaginations. "I always felt Pucci was so strong it was bigger than any one designer," says Janson. "It has a power of its own."

DEMOCRAZIA CRISTIANA

"Emilio [...] could easily have lived 400 years earlier. He looked different, he talked different, he walked different. We called him dinoccolato, *because he had no mass to his body—he was loose, supple, all fluctuations."*
— Oleg Cassini

Emilio Pucci with his dog walking in Florence, 1948.

And yet there is no getting around the fact that the idea originated in the fertile mind of one particular man at one particular time. Which raises two questions: How did he do it? And perhaps more pertinently, why? How did one man without any real training in design understand that clothing could be not just a mirror of social change, but also its instrument, and not just once but again and again?

To understand the answers to these questions is to understand how the past can become the present, and grow into the future. And the only way to begin to arrive at the answers is to begin with a life.

It is a cliché to say that for most successful designers their life is their work—you imagine them in their atelier, Christian Dior in his suits amid his genteel pearl-gray ballroom chairs, or Balenciaga, cloistering himself like a hermit, just a man and his silhouettes—but for Emilio Pucci this was, literally, true: he didn't live to work or even live for his work, but his work reflected, absolutely and on every level, his life. And it would never have happened except for the random events of that life, a set of circumstances that conspired, almost by accident, to produce one of the most important designers of the 20th century.

Indeed, in many ways, it was a fluke that Pucci was a designer at all—that today people hear the word "Pucci" and think "color," or "print," or "liberty," instead of "Florentine nobility." It certainly wasn't the future Emilio's parents envisaged for their eldest son; the very possibility was beyond anyone's wildest imagining. After all, he was the first person in his family to "work" in around a thousand years, as he himself liked to boast. It simply wasn't what aristocrats did.

What they did was what his ancestors had done: they had been cardinals, and leaders of the Florentine republic. A great-great-

Emilio Pucci with Jacques and Genevieve Fath and Mrs. MacPhee in St. Moritz, 1949. Photo: Max (Max Wagner).

Opposite: Emilio Pucci prepares a model for a photo shoot in the Boboli Garden in Florence. The model is wearing printed cotton gabardine Capri pants with the "Monreale" design and a shirt from the Siciliana Collection, ca. 1955. Photo © David Lees/Corbis Historical/Getty Images.

grandfather had been mayor of Florence, and Emilio's father a city councilman. What they did not do was enter a *trade*. Even when Emilio was born in 1914, when the family palazzo was in one of its cycles of decline, there was no sense that he should plan a career that had anything to do with a *product*. If anything, a future that involved skiing (which he excelled at, and which eventually propelled him onto the Italian national team in 1934) seemed most likely. At the University of Milan he majored in agriculture, presumably to prepare himself for the management of the family estate, and in 1935 he won a scholarship to the University of Georgia in America, but there he was inspired by dreams of silver-screen nobility, not the animal husbandry he was nominally studying. Put another way: he wasn't there to learn to birth cattle; he was there to experience life. This will become something of a theme.

A year later Pucci was offered a skiing scholarship to Reed College in Oregon, where he redesigned the team's uniforms and received his Master's degree in history (he later received a doctorate in political science from the University of Florence), but then—heeding the call of duty—he returned home to serve in World War II and became a pilot in the Italian air force. It was during these years that he met Mussolini's daughter, Edda Ciano, whose husband had tried to overthrow her father, and became her lover, eventually helping her escape to Switzerland and as a result ending up in a Nazi jail. Pucci was tortured and close to death before his family managed to get him released and sent to a hospital in Switzerland. When he was well enough he taught Italian and gave skiing lessons to survive.

All of which might not seem like the sort of experiences that would provide fertile ground for a young design mind to grow;

"Coco Chanel was the only one who was nice to me, and so when I created my motor scooter I asked her advice. She suggested I should send it to Germany, so I did, and they copied it. Once my idea of becoming an inventor had passed, I threw myself into making clothes."

— Emilio Pucci

Opposite: Dress with mock bolero bodice in black and white printed cotton, "Tagliatelle" hat, "Mephisto" sandals. Capri, Spring/Summer 1952 Collection.

Emilio Pucci with Susanna Agnelli and friends in Colorado Springs, 1951. Photo: Bob McIntyre.

until, that is, you distill their essence and understand the value of what they teach. For example, the experience of living in a foreign country where dressing in separates was *de rigueur* and you were judged on your own abilities and achievements. For example, learning to appreciate clothing that allowed you to speed unencumbered down a slope. For example, seeing the world in a blur of color and form from high above. For example, risking your life for the love of a woman. And surviving torture, and coming out the other side with a belief that if you could do that, you could do anything.

Such experiences turned out to matter a great deal when it came to the creation of Pucci, the brand—literally, in fact, since the first item of clothing Emilio designed was a ski suit. And it wasn't meant to be sold. It was meant to make his girlfriend more comfortable.

In 1947 Emilio, who had remained in the air force, had returned to Switzerland for a skiing vacation with one of his many paramours. The ski outfits he had first created in Oregon had evolved into stretchy stirrup pants made from a Swiss-manufactured fabric called Helanca (at the time, everyone else was wearing knickerbockers and hose), and in St. Moritz he created matching outfits for himself and his girlfriend. He didn't see why women should have any less physical freedom on the slopes than men, and this gesture toward sartorial gender equality became the beginning of a fashion legend: by chance a young photographer by the name of Toni Frissell, who worked for the powerful American fashion magazine *Harper's Bazaar*, was also skiing, and she took some snaps of the glamorously schussing couple. These made their way back to the desk of fashion editor Diana Vreeland, who in turn called Marjorie Griswold, the head buyer of Lord & Taylor, who called Pucci, and placed an order.

Models on the roof of Palazzo Pucci in Florence, wearing evening dresses, palazzo pajamas and terrycloth capes. Spring/Summer 1967 Collection.

This, then, became another formative lesson for the creative Marchese: an instinct that told him women wanted freedom, sartorially as well as socially, had proved to be right, and could be commercial.

As Carla Sozzani points out, "Pucci didn't have any influences except his own life, friends, and travel. He wasn't a designer in the sense of being absorbed by fashion, he was more of a Renaissance man: he was interested in everything, and could see how it all fit together."

So, logically, what began on the slopes soon extended its reach to swimwear. Pucci went to Capri, then a tiny resort for artists, intellectuals, and a handful of European aristocrats in his circle, and a similar situation presented itself: there was his girlfriend with only big, highly constructed clothes to wear. "Fashion at this time meant a lot of skirts," says Cristina Pucci, whom Emilio married in 1959—and skirts at a beach resort, especially

HARPER'S BAZAAR

NEW YORK 22, N. Y. · 572 MADISON AVENUE

CARMEL SNOW
EDITOR
FRED DRAKE
GENERAL MANAGER

May 26, 1948

Dear Count Pucci:

I have just left Lord and Taylor after seeing your ski clothes. They are excellent. Noone is more thrilled than Miss Griswald. I am sure that she has written you, herself, to say that the ski clothes have arrived and how pleased she is.

Thank you so very much for your letter of May 21.

Very sincerely yours,

DV:cr Diana Vreeland

Count Emilio Pucci di Barsento
Palace Pucci, Via de'Pucci 4
Florence
Ttaly

Two letters from Diana Vreeland, fashion editor for *Harper's Bazaar,* to Emilio Pucci, 1948. Courtesy of Emilio Pucci Archive, Florence.

The first (May 1948) concerns the first shipment of skiwear for Lord & Taylor.

HARPER'S BAZAAR

NEW YORK 22, N.Y. · 572 MADISON AVENUE

CARMEL SNOW
EDITOR
FRED DRAKE
PUBLISHER

October 13, 1948

Dear Marquis Pucci:

I have at last returned to New York and gone through my mail and packages.

First of all, I have to thank you for the perfectly beautiful green damask. Both pieces are such a wonderful color and superb quality. I can never tell you how much I appreciate your generosity and trouble in arranging them and also in sending them to me. Thank you a million times.

Thank you for your article and photographs of the Island Weaver. I have turned this over to Miss McFadden who is in charge of articles and we will probably not use it until next summer. It is interesting and the pictures are very charming. You have gone to a lot of trouble and we certainly appreciate it.

Your ski clothes will appear in the December issue and I will surely see that you see a copy of that issue. Your clothes have been so magnificently copied and Miss Griswold is so ecstatic over the entire thing and I know this will please you enormously. She is a wonderful woman and your clothes are in wonderful hands and will be shown and sold to your best possible advantage.

Do let us know your news from time to time.

With all best luch and again a million thanks.

Very sincerely yours,

Diana Vreeland

Diana Vreeland

DV/by

Marquis Emilio Pucci
Palace Pucci
Via Pucci 4
Florence, Italy

The second (October 1948) is about the article that appeared in *Harper's Bazaar* in December 1948, with images by Toni Frissel.

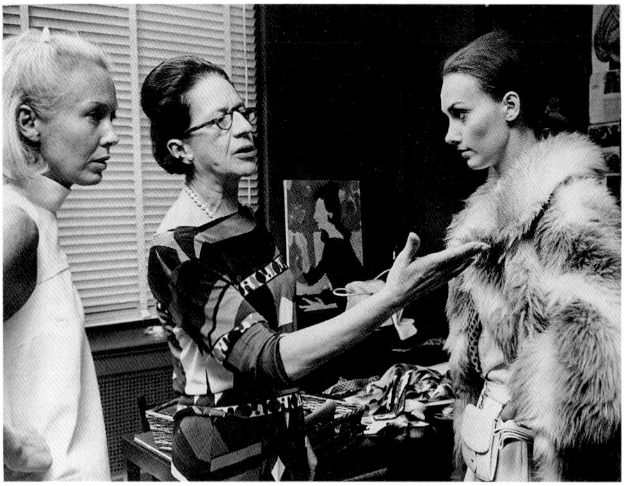

Diana Vreeland, the director of *Vogue* USA, wearing a Pucci dress, photographed in her office with Cathy di Montezemolo and a model, 1960s.
Photo © Scherman/Time-Life.

Opposite: One-piece bathing suit with whalebone bustier and balloon culottes in cotton print with "Palloncini" motif, multicolored straw hat. Spring/Summer 1958 Collection.
Photo: Marchiori, Florence.

one with lots of steps up and down, are not exactly liberating. Men's wear, which is to say, trousers and easy shirts, was liberating. So Emilio made a man's trouser for a woman—as body-conscious as his ski-wear, stretched exactingly over the hips and cropped at the ankle—and paired it with an extremely light-weight silk shirt, both realized in the bright shades found on the island.

And since at this point in his life, Emilio had to work—"His mother had quite a lot of money and his father had money, but after the War and Mussolini it was all gone," explains Laudomia Pucci, Emilio's daughter (who, after his death in 1992, took over the company)—he left the air force and instead opened a tiny store on the island. In order to do it, he subsisted on "one yogurt a day," says Laudomia, and lived in a room in the back of the store. He said, "I owe my career to a woman, so I will make it my job to make them more beautiful." He could also have added: "to make their lives easier, and their closets so much more colorful."

Think about this in context. At that time "fashion" did not really exist *per se*; for the rich, there was couture in Paris and Italy, in the hands of such names as Dior and Capucci, and for everyone else there was the dressmaker down the street or the department-store copies of couture. Ready-to-wear, however, had not yet been born. In Italy, many of the famous fashion names such as Gucci and Ferragamo were still primarily leather-goods manufacturers, selling hand-bags and shoes. Yet here was a store offering a compromise: clothes that would be tailored to your body ("Oh my God, those fittings!" says Laudomia. "One millimeter, two millimeters...") by one of the most dashing men on the island: tanned, tall, thin, in white trousers and a white Cuban shirt.

"The genius of the clothes," says Andrew Bolton, curator of the Metropolitan Museum

To Emilio,
My favorite designer,
With warm regards—
Connie Sharpe

"When I was fifteen and sixteen, I wore Pucci, Pucci, Pucci all the time. Not just the prints, but also shirts and Capri pants all in one color, like pajamas."

— Carla Sozzani

Opposite: Printed and embroidered silk top and loose odalisque silk jersey trousers. Spring/Summer 1964 Collection. The inscription on the photograph reads: "To Emilio, my favorite designer. With warm regards. Connie Sharpe."

Tunic in printed silk twill featuring the "Balinese" motif, with silk jersey odalisque trousers. Fall/Winter 1964 Collection. Earrings and bracelets by Coppola e Toppo for Emilio Pucci. Photo: Gino di Grandi Associates.

of Art's Costume Institute, "was rooted in the fact Emilio Pucci married an Italian sensibility—Diana Vreeland called him 'divinely Italian'—to an American philosophy of sportswear," which together added up to "the *joie de vivre*" as expressed in color and print. In the beginning, the prints were of the island, or fish, or other figurative drawings; later they became more abstract.

But Pucci's family was shocked. "They were quite scandalized when he opened his own boutique; there was one old uncle who just couldn't understand it," remembers Cristina Pucci. "Later they came to appreciate it, because he became famous, and it's hard to reject glamor and fame." Still, they weren't the only ones who initially balked at the idea: many of Emilio's fellow aristocrats were likewise horrified. "He really went his own direction, and didn't care what his social peers were doing or what they thought, and they thought he was doing some very strange stuff. I think there was envy hidden behind those eyes, though," says Pecori Giraldi.

"He had this incredible confidence," remembers Cristina Pucci. He also had a sense of humor. "When he saw his 'friends' coming, he would get out a bucket of water and start scrubbing the floor," says Laudomia Pucci. Still, he cared enough about the family's feelings to name the store Emilio of Capri, to avoid bringing dishonor on the Pucci name. The irony is, of course, that the store brought exactly the opposite.

"Everyone, everyone, wore Pucci in those days," remarks ex–*Vogue* fashion editor Polly Mellen. "You'd see Gianni Agnelli and Brigitte Bardot and they'd be jumping off the boat in their Puccis, and it was just the most glamorous, sexy thing."

"The Americans understood it, and breaking the American market was absolutely key to the success," says Bolton. Between the rich foreigners and the Hollywood stars

Air hostesses of Braniff Airways in Dallas wearing uniforms designed by Emilio Pucci, 1971. Photo © Braniff Collection, Pucci Folder, History of Aviation Collection, Special Collections Department, McDermott Library, The University of Texas at Dallas.

who frequented Capri and the little Emilio shop—the colors looked as good against the beaches of Los Angeles as they did against the beaches of the Mediterranean—suddenly the line had a reach and a renown far beyond its own shores, as did the Florentine Marchese.

"He was a real ambassador for Italian fashion; he totally changed the way the world thought about it," avows Rosita Missoni, scion of the Italian knitwear family. "He was a great communicator, a real pioneer."

By 1950 Pucci had set up shop in the family palazzo, started a proper wholesale business, and begun showing his collections, first during the women's wear week at the Palazzo Pitti (the old Medici palace, and the only house in Florence bigger than the Puccis'), and later in the family ballroom. By 1952, he was earning enough to start restoring the family home. By the late 1950s he was a genuine phenomenon.

Opposite: Palazzo pajamas with silk chiffon cape featuring the "Lance" panel motif fastened by an embroidered necklace and turquoise silk crêpe catsuit, with oriental trousers fastened on the ankles by embroidered bands. Embroidered skullcap and gem-encrusted sandals by Coppola e Toppo. Photo: Gian Paolo Barbieri, courtesy of Fondazione Gian Paolo Barbieri ETS, © Giada Barbieri.

Emilio Pucci and two models during a rehearsal for a fashion show in London, 1963. Photo: David Hurn for John Hillelson Agency Ltd.

When I was fifteen and sixteen, I wore Pucci, Pucci, Pucci all the time," says Carla Sozzani. "Not just the prints, but also shirts and Capri pants all in one color, like pajamas. I spent so much of my parents' money on Pucci my father got upset."

"In 1965 I remember going on my first trip to New York for the inauguration of the ship *Michelangelo*," says Rosita Missoni. "My parents had asked me to accompany them as a translator—and all of the windows on Fifth Avenue were full of Pucci. They were copies, of course."

Indeed, there were so many copies that Lord & Taylor's Marjorie Griswold suggested Pucci should begin signing his work, and hence the scripted "Emilio" was worked into every print, and the logo was born. Because the clothes were meant for life—"for women who ran around in flat shoes and had to get the children," according to Pecori Giraldi—the shapes were incredibly simple and unrestrictive. "For my father, the body of the woman moved the dress, the dress didn't create the body of the woman," says Laudomia. But at the same time, of course, they flattered the shape. In the palazzo, the Marchese would fit his clothes not just on one model, as is standard, but on two or three, to ensure the shape was flattering no matter what the body type. "He used to say he didn't dress a woman, he dressed all women," says Laudomia. Actually, however, the women he dressed were his friends, and the clothes he made were inspired by their needs. "I wear a lot of black," says Otto today. "And if I'm not wearing black, I'm usually in Pucci, which would seem to be the direct opposite, but I realized what I like about both is the same: they are easy. With Pucci, you put it on, and you don't need anything else: no accessories, no outfit."

Just as he created a uniform for the beach and a uniform for the slopes, he made a

"Someone who comes from a family that somehow survived for a thousand years in a city like Florence, among intrigues and conspiracies, must possess stronger than average qualities: for instance, moral resilience."
— Emilio Pucci

Emilio Pucci during the fitting of a trouser suit with a printed chenille poncho featuring the "Taitù" motif for the Fall/Winter 1963/64 Collection. Photo: David Hurn for John Hillelson Agency Ltd.

uniform to travel in. In conjunction with manufacturer Mario Boselli, he developed an incredibly light and thin stretch jersey that could be folded up into a tiny square. "It dared to imagine a life of freedom where you didn't have to travel with a maid to iron your clothes every night. In this sense, it prefigured many changes in women's lives, and it's this vision that is still relevant today," says Holly Brubach, ex–fashion editor of the *New Yorker* and style editor of the *New York Times* magazine. Then, because life is not limited to clothing, he also designed towels, sheets, rugs, even the labels for a wine he produced in his country estate—not to mention, in later years, a car, stewardess uniforms, and the logo for the Apollo 15 space shuttle. Peter Dundas, artistic director of Pucci from 2008 to 2015, says: "It was not about style; it was about lifestyle." And this was reflected not only in the functionality of the clothing, whether an evening pajama or a little jersey dress, but literally, in the clothing itself—or rather, the prints on the clothing.

For these colorful, alluring designs—"doodles, really," as Peter Dundas says—reflected the historical interests and life of Emilio Pucci himself. In those drawings you can see the curving roof of the Duomo opposite his top-floor window and the mosaics from the floor, the scrollwork on the iron gates of the palazzo, the flags of the competing city zones represented in the Palio of Siena, shooting stars, and waterfalls. The irony is, however, that they were so enchanting and so iconic they soon began to obscure the stories they contained, to the extent that they have become almost a brand for the brand. Because while so many people reflexively think Pucci is about prints, the truth is, the prints are about Pucci. "I think he saw his drawing as figurative," says Laudomia. "I think of it as a readable abstract."

Emilio Pucci at the Canzone del Mare Beach in Capri, 1952.

Opposite: Emilio Pucci, winner of the Neiman Marcus Award 1955 in Dallas, with Ivy Nicholson wearing a print silk twill shirt, with "Mosaico" motif, and shantung silk Capri pants.

In some ways, the prints even contributed to the brand's fallow period. By the 1970s, pretty was out and social unrest was in, and, says Stefano Tonchi, former editor of the *New York Times* style supplements, who grew up in Florence at the time. "In the 1970s and '80s, Italy was really split between the Left and the Right, and no self-respecting Leftist would wear Pucci, as it was so associated with society and the jet set."

Pucci fell out of favor, although the Marchese continued to work, and his aesthetics continued to inspire numerous other designers, including Versace, Dolce & Gabbana, and Diane von Furstenberg, the latter of whom says: "He influenced me a lot, with the idea that dressing should be easy, and that it should fill a purpose, so you never feel you don't have anything to wear." Still, it took another generation before Pucci was rediscovered.

"By the mid-1980s, I remember going to discos and suddenly seeing these girls in print leggings, and they looked like the coolest people in the room. It suddenly went from seemingly conservative to seemingly totally hip," says Tonchi. "In a way, it was so out of fashion it was ripe to come back in." The vintage market boomed, because, as Cameron Silver, owner of the California vintage store Decades says, "Pucci showed vintage was not about costume, because the designs were so modern."

"In a way, because the forms were so simple, they have really held up in terms of fashion," says Bolton.

"The thing you realize about vintage Pucci," says Pecori Giraldi, "is you put it on and it looks absolutely right. Often with vintage you look at it as an object: a wonderful symbol of what happened 30 years ago, but not something you'd ever wear today. Capucci is like this—when the hell do you wear it? Pucci, on the other hand, you can just throw on and wear every single day."

Pages 44/45: Christian Lacroix and his team with Laudomia Pucci selecting prints for the Spring/Summer 2003 Collection. Photo © Jean-Noel De Soye/FigaroPhoto.com.

Peter Dundas, who was then creative director of the Pucci Company, with a model during a fitting in Palazzo Pucci headquarters, Florence, 2009. Photo: Santi Caleca.

By 1989, although he was over 70, Pucci was back on top. As Suzy Menkes, former fashion editor of the *International Herald Tribune*, wrote: "Everything is coming up Pucci." The idea still worked. "Early in the 1980s, during his revival, when I first joined the company to work with him, he was making these catsuits, and I said 'What are you doing? No one will wear that!'" remembers Laudomia. "And my father said, 'Yes, they will.' He was in his mid-70s at the time. And he was absolutely right." The catsuits made it into *Vogue*.

When the Marchese had to retire for health reasons, Laudomia, who had worked closely with him over the years, carried on his work, collaborating behind the scenes with various designers from Stephan Janson to Antonio Berardi. But although the core principles of Pucci held, the world was changing—globalization had kicked in, and luxury was listed on various stock exchanges. It eventually became clear that the family needed a bigger infrastructure behind it if it were to continue disseminating and building on what the Marchese had created, and in the year 2000 a majority stake of the company was sold to LVMH, with Laudomia continuing as Image Director, responsible for maintaining the link between past and future. Of all the clothing lines that had started in post war Italy, Pucci was the only one still in existence. Why? The idea.

"Pucci is an iconic brand: instantly recognizable, and possessed of a distinctive message; fun, practical, sporty, incredibly innovative and very leading-edge," says Bernard Arnault, chairman and chief executive of LVMH, explaining why he wanted to add the Italian label to a stable that already included the French houses Louis Vuitton, Givenchy, and Celine, and the Spanish brand Loewe (among many others). "It was also clean," he continues—despite the many brand exten-

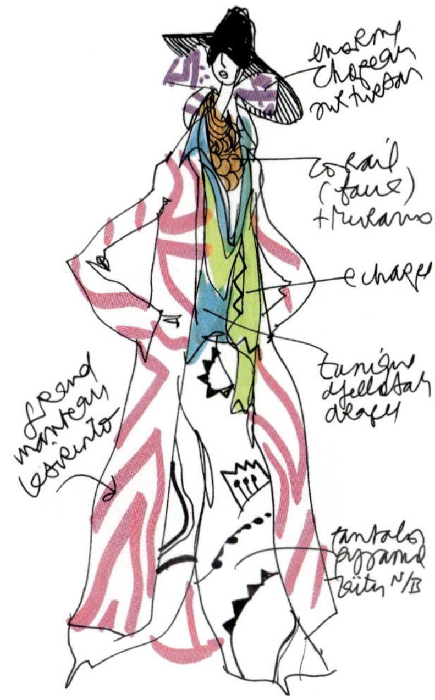

Sketch for Fall/Winter 2003 Collection, by Christian Lacroix for Emilio Pucci. Pen and marker on paper. Spring/Summer 2003 Collection. *Flair,* June 2003.

sions, it had never become devalued as had, say, Pierre Cardin—"capable of growth, and what I would describe as a sleeping beauty." So he set about waking it up.

The first step was to hire a designer to take the brand forward and, along with Laudomia, who provided continuity and ballast in the face of change, to act as a creative force for the company. First this was the Puerto Rican Julio Espada, soon followed by Christian Lacroix, who says, "It mustn't remain a prisoner of the past, even a fertile past, not content itself with caricaturing the 'dolce vita' glamor of what we called café society before the jet set.

"I was quite delighted to be asked to come to the brand, because I found that it was legitimate and unpretentious to think about me for Pucci. In fact, I had thought about it when the group had acquired the fashion house which, from a cultural point of view, I was very fond of. I had drawn and redrawn 'Pucci' style patterns again and again with my first felt-tip pens. Later on, in the 1980s, my wife and I bought vintage Pucci in the London or Paris flea markets, and I had even paid tribute to the Marchese in one of my first 'luxury' ready-to-wear collections."

Lacroix's Pucci was a riot of prints and sportswear diversification, and landed the brand back on the catwalk radar. "I loved it," says André Leon Talley, former editor-at-large of American *Vogue.* "The colors! The lifestyle!" After his eponymous brand was sold by LVMH in 2005, however, Lacroix moved on and was replaced by the English designer Matthew Williamson, who also brought his own ideas to the brand while respecting the past, just as Emilio had done, by using his historical touchstones as inspiration for his prints.

"It was really thrilling," remembers Williamson, "because my background is as a textile designer. One journalist, when I

Sketches for Fall/Winter 2003 Collection, by Christian Lacroix for Emilio Pucci. Pen and marker on paper. Spring/Summer 2003 Collection. *Flair*, June 2003.

Pages 50/51: Printed silk georgette long dress in the "Maschere" motif. Spring/Summer 2003 Collection. *Flair*, June 2003. Photo © Patrick Demarchelier/Flair Mondadori.

got the job, said 'This is like leading Charlie to the Chocolate Factory,' and it was. I was really attracted to the way it looked like painting on canvas, and the fluidity of the fabric." He also integrated the brand with his social life, which revolved around a group of young hip girls, just as the original Pucci had mined his own social connections for ideas.

To put it another way, both Lacroix and Williamson dipped into the house's DNA, and brought a different trait to the fore according to their personal preferences and experiences. And then, in 2008, as the world entered recession and the house another phase, a new designer took the helm: Norwegian Peter Dundas, whose first collection returned to Emilio Pucci's Palio collection of 1957 for inspiration, and then transformed it for the jet-set girls of today. He was followed by the Italian Massimo Giorgetti in 2015, who was the creative director until 2017, before leaving the creation of the new collections in the hands of an in-house team.

In many ways, the brand has come full circle. As Rust said, in the noughties "Every woman in a certain Manhattan zip code has their favorite happy Pucci dress," just as they did in the 1950s. As a brand, Pucci "represents the rebirth of optimism," says Silver, and that is particularly relevant as the world—its world—experiences the worst economic climate in decades.

Before he passed away, Emilio Pucci said to his wife, "Don't let my work die." Later Carrie Donovan, then the *New York Times* fashion editor, pronounced of Pucci, "He personified a moment." And although she qualified it by adding "a rather long one," the truth is, history has proved her completely, gloriously, wrong. Silhouettes have to do with moments. Ideas, on the other hand, and Pucci are forever.

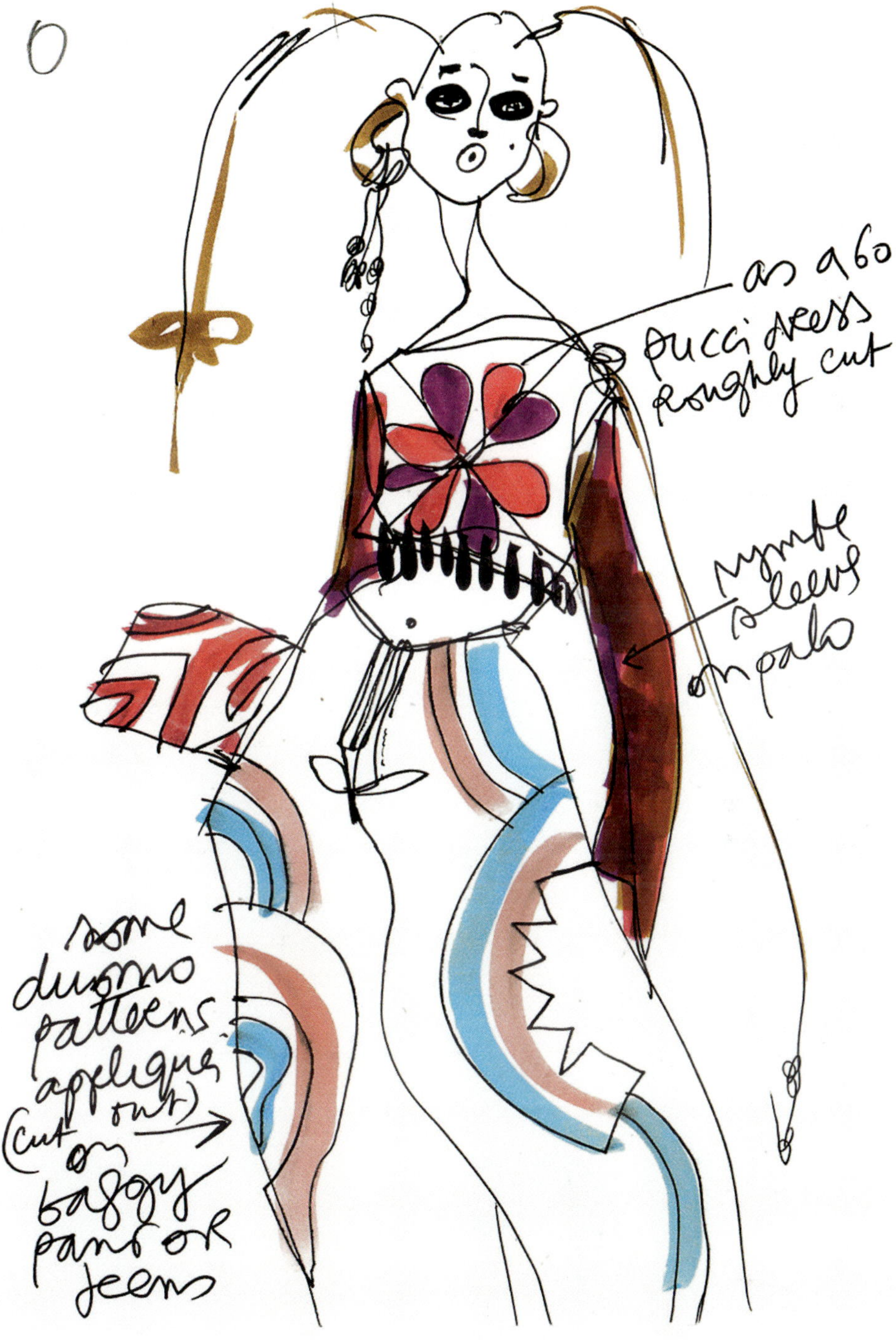
as a 60
Pucci dress
roughly cut
some
patterns
applique
(cut out)
on
baggy
pants or
jeans

"He wanted to give women freedom, joy, make them as beautiful as possible."

— Laudomia Pucci

Of Country and Culture

"No man is an island," wrote John Donne, and similarly no act of creation comes from a vacuum; visions are born of place and past, and this is no less true of a global brand than a fresco or a sculpture. Despite its international reach and ability to speak to multiple groups, Italy and its traditions were woven into the colors, fabric, and forms of Emilio Pucci, and even though in recent years a Puerto Rican, a Frenchman, an Englishman, and a Norwegian, then another Italian have sat in the chair where the Marchese once reigned, the first thing they have understood is that surroundings matter. You just have to understand where to look.

Emilio Pucci seated in front of a display of scarfs from the Palio Collection (1957) and the Botticelliana Collection (1959). The model is wearing an evening dress with whalebone bustier and heart-shaped neckline in printed silk twill, featuring the "Padiglione" scarf motif. Forte Belvedere, Florence, 1959.
Photo © David Lees/Corbis Historical/Getty Images.

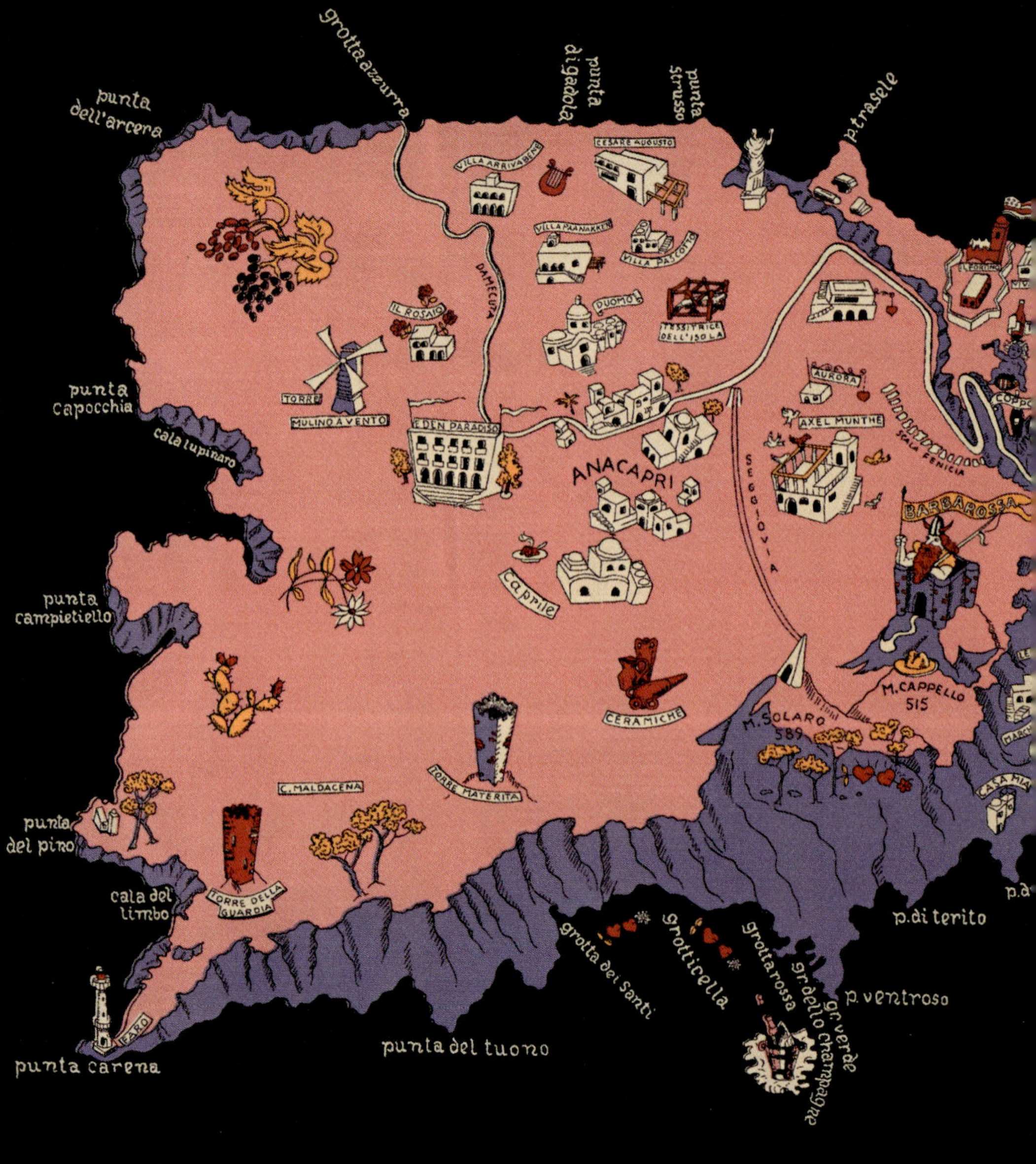

grotta azzurra
punta di gadola
punta strusso
p. trasele
punta dell'arcera
VILLA ARRIVABENE
CESARE AUGUSTO
VILLA PASCOTTO
DUOMO
TESSITRICE DELL'ISOLA
IL ROSAIO
DAMECUTA
AURORA
AXEL MUNTHE
SCALA FENICIA
punta capocchia
cala lupinaro
TORRE
MULINO A VENTO
EDEN PARADISO
ANACAPRI
SEGGIOVIA
BARBAROSSA
Caprile
punta campietiello
CERAMICHE
M. CAPPELLO
515
M. SOLARO
589
C. MALDACENA
TORRE MATERITA
punta del piro
cala del limbo
TORRE DELLA GUARDIA
FARO
punta carena
punta del tuono
grotta dei santi
grotticella
grotta rossa
gr. dello champagne
gr. verde
p. ventroso
p. di terito
CASA MIA

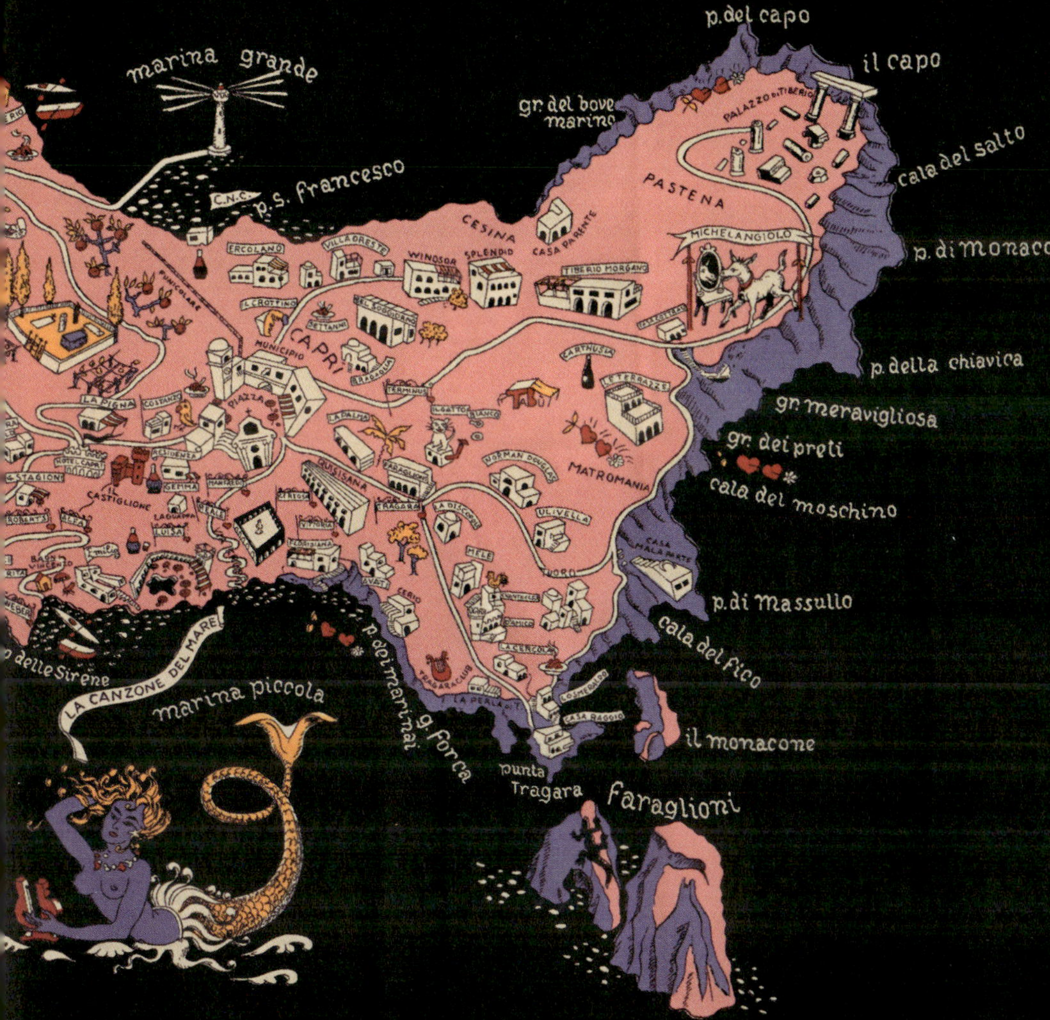

marina grande
C.N.C.
p.s. francesco
p.del capo
il capo
gr. del bove marino
PALAZZO DI TIBERIO
cala del salto
PASTENA
CESINA
CASA PARENTE
p. di Monaco
MICHELANGIOLO
TIBERIO MORGANO
SPLENDID
WINDSOR
VILLA ORESTE
ERCOLANO
FUNICOLARE
CAPRI
MUNICIPIO
PIAZZA
LA PIGNA
CARTHUSIA
LE TERRAZZE
TERMINUS
p. della chiavica
gr. meravigliosa
gr. dei preti
MATROMANIA
NORMAN DOUGLAS
cala del moschino
QUISISANA
TRAGARA
ULIVELLA
CASTIGLIONE
CASA MALAPARTE
CERIO
p. di Massullo
cala del fico
LA CERCOLA
CASA RAGGIO
TRAGARA CLUB
il monacone
punta Tragara
Faraglioni
g. Forca
p. dei marinai
marina piccola
LA CANZONE DEL MARE
p. delle Sirene

"Emilio Pucci was fascinated by his roots, and art and architecture; you can actually see it in his work. On my honeymoon in Capri in 1953 I remember going to his shop and being struck by how much the designs resembled Florentine mosaics. It was really extraordinary, although I don't think a lot of people realized it."

— Rosita Missoni

Pages 54/55: Detail of the "Isola di Capri" scarf, featuring a map with the most attractive tourist spots on the island, 1952. Silk twill, 90 x 90 cm.

Left: Caftan in white silk twill with ruffles featuring the "Nisida" motif. Spring/Summer 2018 Collection. Model: Valery Kaufman.
Photo © Mel Bles/Webber Represents.

Opposite: Shaded silk taffeta polka-dot evening dress embellished with strass and pearls, whalebone bustier with heart-shaped neckline and loose skirt. Matching headpiece embellished with pearls; necklace, earrings and sandals. Spring/Summer 1955 Collection.

Cotton shirt and printed cotton trousers, featuring the "Riccioli" motif and straw hat. Spring/Summer 1955 Collection.

Opposite top: A sketch of fhe Capri boutique at the Canzone del Mare Beach, 1950. China ink on card, 11 x 18 cm.

Opposite bottom: Pareo trousers, wrap-around silk shantung shirt tied over the hip, conical straw hat and "Mephisto" sandals. Spring/Summer 1952 Collection. Ivy Nicholson poses in front of the Capri boutique, 1951. Photo: Relang, Munich.

Emilio
Emilio

Printed silk twill shirt and trousers suit.
Spring/Summer 1955 Collection, Capri.
Photo: Lumachi.

Shantung silk striped shirt with pinstripe cotton Capri pants, "Scarabocchio" straw hat and sandals, 1954. Ivy Nicholson.
Photo: Scrimali.

Opposite: Red cotton canvas trousers and cotton shirt with white and pink stripes, "Soli" scarf wrapped around the waist, large-brimmed straw hat, sandals, 1954. Ivy Nicholson.
Photo: Scrimali.

Sketch for a beachwear outfit: blue and coral cotton buttoned top with wide skirt and blue cotton belt, to be worn over a one-piece coral swimsuit, wide-brimmed hat and straw handbag. Spring/Summer 1954 Collection. Pencil and tempera on paper, 25 x 35 cm.

"It was the years of the Cinecittà, and Rome and Italy were an influential force. It was the famous time of La Dolce Vita. *I think this actually helped with the American market, because the United States and Italy had understood each other since the beginning of the 20th century because of their shared affinity for the cinema, the sweet things and the comforts of life, their taste for luxury and modernity."*

— Christian Lacroix

Opposite: Fragment of gray and gold hand-painted fabric with a view of Capri, 1954.

Don Emilio Pucci in Capri with Princess Maria Pia of Savoy and other friends. The Princess is wearing a Pucci outfit with printed silk twill shirt and skirt featuring motifs from the Sicilian Collection, 1956. Photo: Roberto.

From top to bottom:
Label: "Emilio S.r.L.," 1953.

Design for label "Capri Sports S.r.L.," 1951. China ink on tracing paper, 13 x 6 cm.

Design for label "Capri Sports S.r.L.," 1951. China ink on paper, 13 x 4 cm.

Opposite: Knitted top featuring an embroidery inspired by the Emilio Pucci historic tag representing the Faraglioni of Capri. Resort 2018 Collection. Model: Aira Ferreira.
Photo © Maciek Kobielski.

S.R.L
MADE IN ITAL
CAPRI

"The environment he lived in gave him so much. There was so much to look at!"

— André Leon Talley

Opposite: Emilio Pucci on the terrace of the Canzone del Mare Beach in Capri, 1952.

"Piazzetta di Capri" scarf, 1950s. Silk twill, 84 x 84 cm.

C
Capri. La Canzone del mare.
F
Firenze Via dei Pucci 4 ☎ 27.622.
R
Roma Via Campania 59 ☎ 488.817.

Opposite top: Drawing containing addresses of the boutiques in Capri, Florence, and Rome, 1950s.
Print on card, 10 x 15 cm.

Opposite bottom: Printed cotton shirt with "Scorci capresi" motif.
Fall/Winter 1950/51 Collection.

"Canzone del Mare" scarf, 1950s.
Silk twill, 89 x 89 cm.

"Positano" scarf, 1950s.
Silk twill, 90 x 90 cm.

Opposite: Detail of the caption of the map of the island of Capri on the "Isola di Capri" scarf, 1952.
Silk twill, 90 x 90 cm.

Leggenda
HOTEL
Qui si
Qui si
Qui si
Qui si
Qui si
Qui si
Qui si ....
Emilio
Qui si

Hooded shirt in aqua-blue silk sateen with shantung silk oriental skirt, sandals. Spring/Summer 1952 Collection, Capri, Villa Settanni.
Photo: G. Herter.

Opposite: Stella Tennant wears an evening dress in aqua-colored printed silk jersey. Printed silk scarf featuring the "Riviera" motif, black leather sandals. Spring/Summer 2009 Collection, Sorrento.
Photo © Juergen Teller.

"You only have to go to Florence to see how important it was to the development of Pucci: his colors, his inspiration, all begins there."

— Delphine Arnault

Opposite: Drawing for "Duomo" print motif. Fall/Winter 2007 Collection.

"Duomo 2" scarf, 1974.
Silk twill, 90 x 90 cm.

"Florence as a city was very important to Emilio. He was a member of parliament twice, and very involved in the politics of Florence. He really wanted to make it the best city possible." — Cristina Pucci

"Battistero" scarf, 1950s.
Silk twill, 90 x 90 cm.

Opposite: The installation "Monumental Pucci" on the occasion of "Firenze Hometown of Fashion," 2014. The baptistery is covered by a giant reproduction of a scarf originally designed by Emilio Pucci in the 1950s.
Photo Stefano Trovati/© SGP.

"We have that kind of optimism in the brand and a real sense of happiness. It's about capturing these beautiful moments. The clothes are feminine, they express themselves through colors and prints, which adds an artistic dimension to them, and they are at their heart, Italian."

— Laudomia Pucci

Both pages: Printed cotton handkerchiefs inspired by Giuseppe Zocchi's 18th-century prints with views of Florence. Cotton batiste, 45 x 45 cm.

Opposite: The Pitti Palace. It was used for the electoral campaign of Emilio Pucci for the Italian Liberal Party.

The Santa Trinita bridge.

"Duomo 1" scarf, 1968.
Silk twill, 90 x 90 cm.

Opposite: "Primavera (Medici)" scarf, inspired by the celebrations for 500 years of the Medici family in Florence, 1980. Silk twill, 90 x 90 cm.

"He liked Old Masters: Fra Angelico, Botticelli, early Renaissance painters. It all came back to where he was born. He never even talked to me about Venetian painters, only Tuscan. He didn't even like Titian. The women were too heavy."

— Cristina Pucci

Opposite: Emilio Pucci during the "Calcio in costume" parade. Photo: Locchi, Florence.

"Calcio in costume" scarf, 1955. Silk twill, 87 x 87 cm.

Printed silk twill shirt featuring
the "Malachite" scarf motif.
Spring/Summer 1959 Collection.

Shantung silk shirt and checkered velvet trousers, small felt toque. Fall/Winter 1954 Collection, Palazzo Pucci. Photo: Relang, Munich.

Opposite: Printed silk coat and silk twill trousers featuring the "Piume" motif. Pre-Fall 2016 Collection. Model: Lia Pavlova. Photo © Alessio Bolzoni.

"Porticato" scarf, 1963.
Cotton gabardine, 90 x 90 cm.

Opposite: Printed silk twill top from the "Porticato" scarf, and shantung silk sarong skirt. Spring/ Summer Haute Couture 1963 Collection. Photo: Relang, Munich.

Opposite: Pajama palazzo suit in printed silk twill, with "Astrolabio" motif. Spring/Summer 1964 Collection. Photo: Lumachi.

"Astrolabio" scarf, 1964. Silk twill, 89 x 89 cm.

"The tension is what made the house: Pucci was turned toward the future, but he never lost sight of tradition. It was innate with him, it was in his blood, his rank, and his ancestors."

— Christian Lacroix

Opposite: Mini dress with printed silk crêpe pleated skirt featuring the "Arlecchino" panel motif and printed Helanca leggings, from the Paggio Collection. Fall/Winter 1965 Collection, Palazzo Pucci, Florence.

Models wearing printed Lycra catsuits with the "Scacchiera" motif, on the roof of Palazzo Pucci. Spring/Summer 1991 Collection. *House and Garden*, January 1991. Photo © Oberto Gili/ House and Garden.

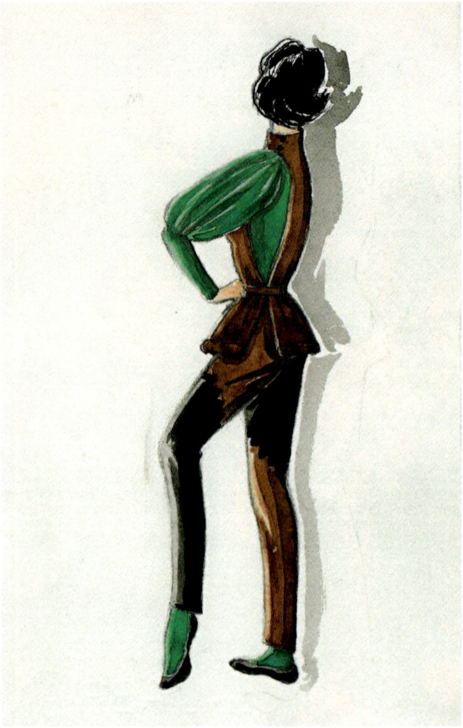

Pages 96–99: Sketches for Renaissance-inspired outfits for the Fall/Winter 1957/58 Collection. Pencil and tempera on paper, 16 x 22 cm.

Above left: Outfit with puffy sleeves, tunic in the Renaissance style with short skirt and two-tone trousers.

Above right: Outfit with gray velvet tunic with decorative patterned edges and velvet trousers.

Opposite: Outfit with tunic and blue velvet trousers.

casacca autunnale

Opposite: Low-cut top and matching shorts.

Above left: Tunic beach-robe, from the Palio Collection; Spring/ Summer 1957.

Above right: Tunic, trousers and jacket with knitted edges, skirt.

"If we were here, every August we went to the Palio in Siena, which was a horse race dating back to the 14th century, involving a great pageant based around seventeen different zones of the city and their colors. It was a tradition, and for Emilio, it was a passion. He made a very famous collection based on it in 1957."

— Cristina Pucci

Après-ski outfit with knit tunic and checkered velvet trousers.

Opposite: Emilio Pucci with models wearing shirts from the Palio Collection in front of the Duomo in Siena, 1957. Photo: Lee Thody.

“There’s an exuberance to the clothes that is very Italian.”

— Holly Brubach

Ensemble of printed silk chiffon evening gown with matching Helanca catsuit featuring the “Rombi” motif. Spring/Summer 1966 Collection, Sardinia, Italy. Photo © Henry Clarke/ Condé Nast Collection/Getty Images.

Multicolored velvet dresses inspired by heraldic motifs. Palio Collection. Fall/Winter 1956. Photo: Lee Thody.

Opposite: Wool gabardine cigarette pants, light three-tone wool top. Fall/Winter 1956 Collection. Photo: Lumachi, Florence.

"In the 1950s the designs were almost jingoistic, they were so referential to Italian history. The graphic elements came from the idea of all these aristocratic families and their flags."

— Andrew Bolton

Pages 106–109: Sketches inspired by heraldic and Renaissance motifs for designs for the Palio Collection, Spring/Summer 1957. Pencil and tempera on paper, 16 x 22 cm.

Opposite: Cocktail dress with a wide full skirt decorated with heraldic motifs.

Above left: One-piece swimming shorts and bolero with printed cotton shawl collar.

Above right: Brown velvet daywear dress with a wide full skirt.

Above left: One-piece swimsuit with shorts and printed cotton flared top buttoned down the back.

Above right: Two-tone tunic beach-robe with scalloped edge.

Opposite: Tunic beach-robe with side buttons and decorative heraldic motif.

I. E.

Emilio Pucci with a model on the roof of Palazzo Pucci in Florence. The model is wearing a silk twill printed shirt and a matching full skirt with the "Giraffa" motif. Palio Collection, Spring/Summer 1957.
Photo: Relang, Munich.

Below left and right: Sketches for costumes for the Alfieri della Contrada del Montone parade at the Palio di Siena.

Opposite: Long strapless dress with full skirt in printed cotton popeline, with fabrics from the different districts: Civetta, Lupa, Montone, Chiocciola, Giraffa, Torre, Bruco, Oca. From the Palio Collection, Spring/Summer 1957.
Pages 111–123 Photo: Paolo Bacherini.

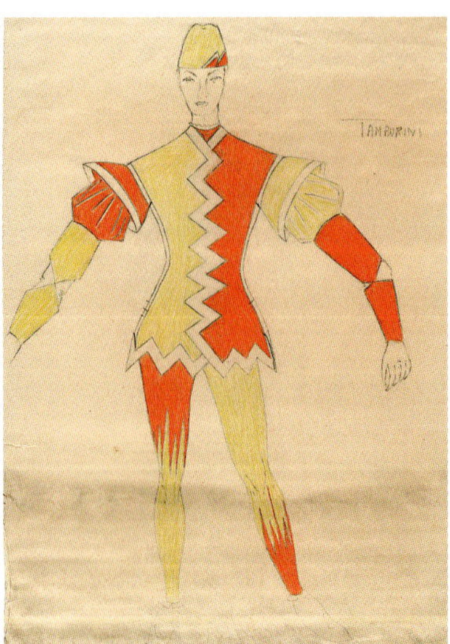

Strapless dress in printed cotton batiste, featuring the "Aquila" motif. From the Palio Collection, Spring/ Summer 1957.

Long strapless dress in printed cotton sateen, featuring the "Civetta" motif. From the Palio Collection, Spring/Summer 1957.

Sleeveless dress with straps, low waist and full skirt with overskirt in printed cotton sateen, with the "Lupa" motif. From the Palio Collection, Spring/Summer 1957.

Outfit with shirt and shorts in printed cotton popeline featuring the "Lupa" motif. From the Palio Collection, Spring/Summer 1957.

Tunic bathrobe in printed cotton sateen, and printed cotton gabardine shorts, featuring the "Onda" motif. From the Palio Collection, Spring/Summer 1957.

Long-sleeve shirt in printed silk twill featuring the "Torre" motif, with black and white shorts. From the Palio Collection, Spring/Summer 1957.

Sleeveless dress with straps, in printed cotton sateen, featuring the "Drago" motif; low waist, wide skirt and overskirt. From the Palio Collection, Spring/Summer 1957.

Strapless dress with balloon skirt in printed silk twill, featuring the "Aquila" motif. From the Palio Collection, Spring/Summer 1957.

Loose trouser-skirt in printed cotton popeline featuring the "Leocorno" motif, shirt in shantung silk. From the Palio Collection, Spring/Summer 1957.

A beachwear outfit with a mini dress and matching printed cotton sateen shorts, featuring the "Lupa" motif. From the Palio Collection, Spring/Summer 1957.

Shorts in printed silk twill featuring the "Civetta" motif, and wide V-neck wool sweater. From the Palio Collection, Spring/Summer 1957.

Cigarette pants in printed cotton canvas featuring the "Civetta" motif, with fringed black wool top. From the Palio Collection, Spring/Summer 1957.

"Understanding the significance of the Palio Collection to the evolution of the brand gave me license to use the past in giving the Pucci girl a face of today." — Peter Dundas

Opposite: Printed cotton terrycloth poncho beach-robe, featuring "Sirena" motifs, multicolored straw hats, "Mephisto" sandals and fishnet shoes in kid leather. Siciliana Collection, Spring/Summer 1955.
Photo © Carlo Torazza.

"Tartuca" scarf from the Palio Collection, 1957. Silk crêpe, 90 x 90 cm.

Opposite: Emilio Pucci with a model wearing a silk shirt featuring the "Finimenti siciliani" motif and cotton trousers. From the Siciliana Collection, Spring/Summer 1955.

"Noto": outfit with silk "mediterranei" trousers printed with the "Finimenti siciliani" motif, cotton shirt. Model Lilli Cerasoli poses in front of a painted Sicilian cart. Photo: Lumachi.

"There is something about the boldness of his color sense that is very Italian: bright and joyful, as if they come from a sunny place."

— Andrew Bolton

Christmas card featuring a siren on a Sicilian cart between Sicily and Capri, 1950s. China ink on tracing paper, 18 x 27 cm.

Opposite: "Finimenti siciliani" fabric, 1955; silk sateen.

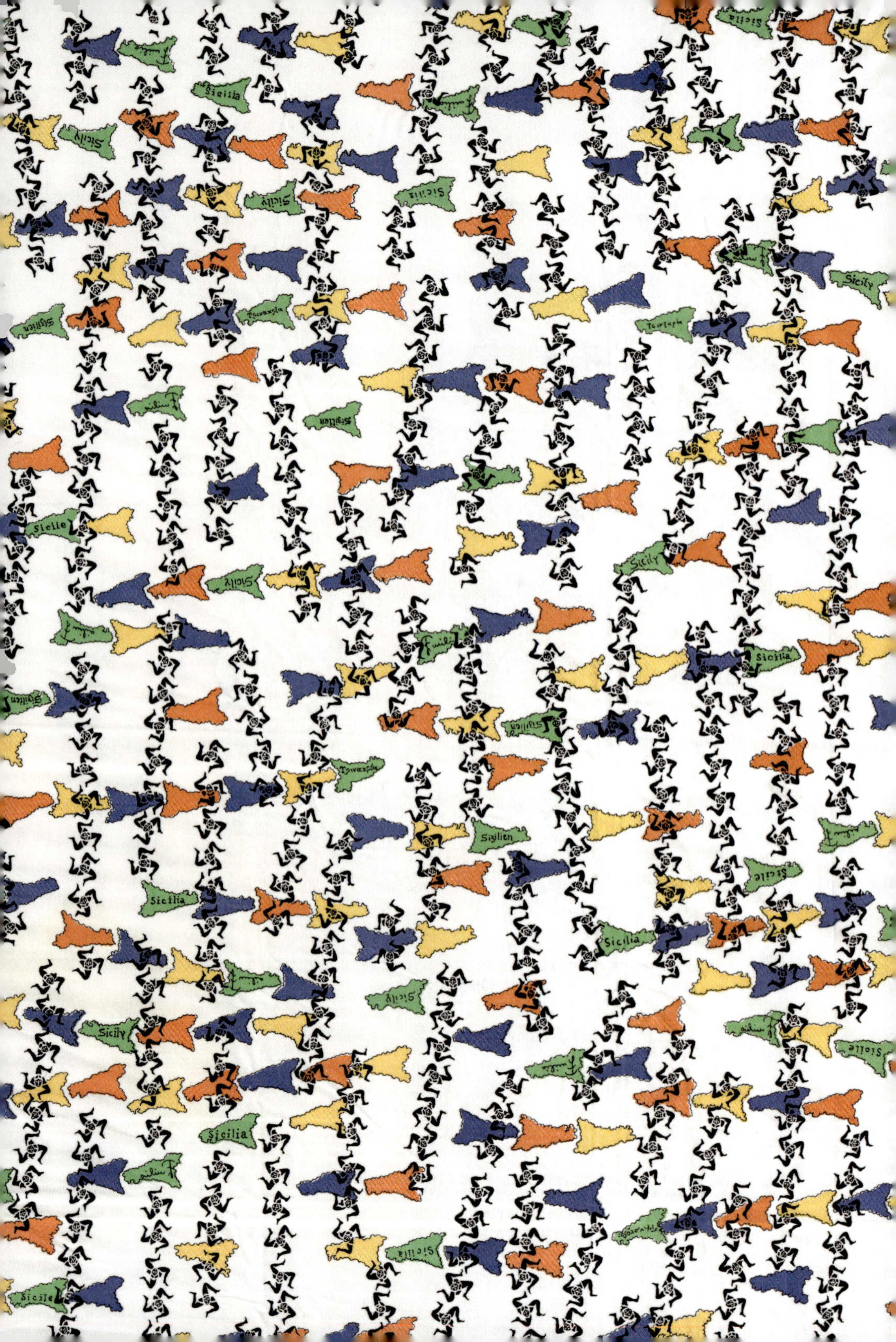

Opposite: "Trinacria Siciliana" fabric, 1955; cotton gabardine.

Cotton bikini, from the Siciliana Collection, Spring/Summer 1955. The model is posing on mosaics depicting "bikini"-clad dancers in Piazza Armerina, Sicily.

One-piece swimsuit with whalebone bustier and draping culottes in hand-painted cotton, featuring the "Pennellate" motif, and multicolored straw hat. Spring/Summer 1956 Collection.

One-piece swimsuit with whalebone bustier and draping culottes in printed and hand-painted cotton, natural straw hat. Spring/Summer 1956 Collection. Model: Lilli Cerasoli.

Outfit with shirt and shorts in printed cotton featuring the "Monreale" motif. This design was inspired by the decorative motifs on the columns of the cloister of Monreale, in Sicily. Siciliana Collection, Spring/Summer 1955.
Photo: Elsa Haertter.

Opposite: Maria Carla Boscono wears a silk jersey evening dress printed with the "Cristallo" motif and colored sunglasses. Fall/Winter 2008/09 Collection.
Photo © Juergen Teller.

Amy Winehouse is seen at "Fashion Rocks," 2007, wearing a sequined mini dress with the "Ceramiche" motif. Fall/Winter 2006/07 Collection. Photo © Bruce Weber.

Opposite: Marilyn Monroe wears a dress by Emilio Pucci in silk jersey printed with the "Ceramiche" motif, 1962. Photo © Bert Stern.

"He did a lot to help the image of Italy internationally—in a way he represented it to all these people whom he knew and he dressed, whether it was Jacqueline Kennedy Onassis or Marilyn Monroe—and he worked very hard at it." — Stefano Tonchi

You Draw What You See

Possibly the greatest misconception about Emilio Pucci is that the prints that made the brand famous are abstract. In fact, they are drawings, often simply inspired by objects, or Pucci's home surroundings. To open the door of the House of Pucci is to open the door to a world of understanding, where suddenly squiggles are revealed as the baroque curves of a wrought-iron gate, and interlocking circles a view of the Duomo from the roof of the Palazzo.

Brass doorknob with the Pucci family crest and other decorative elements, Palazzo Pucci, Florence.
Photo: Santi Caleca.

"You have to realize Emilio Pucci was in a very privileged position, living in a beautiful home full of frescoes; for someone with both fancy and talent, it's a fantastic place to be from. Just his surroundings gave him so much."

— Rosita Missoni

Pages 140/141: "Villa Toscana" scarf, 1950s. Silk twill, 90 x 90 cm.

Opposite: Wrought iron gate with the Pucci family crest at the entrance to Palazzo Pucci in Florence.

Detail of the "Grate di Bronzo" scarf, 1966 (inspired by the motifs on the gate of Palazzo Pucci). Silk twill, 90 x 90 cm.

"Alabarde" scarf, 1980.
Silk twill, 90 x 90 cm.

Opposite: "Struzzo" scarf, 1977.
Silk twill, 90 x 90 cm.

"Everything you need to understand Emilio Pucci is in the palazzo; you just have to think about a different way of seeing what is around you. Take a coat of arms, for example, or another historical pattern, and then think of it drawn freestyle. He was translating the history that was all around him into his work, with doodles."

— Peter Dundas

"Plumages" scarf, 1973.
Silk twill, 90 x 90 cm.

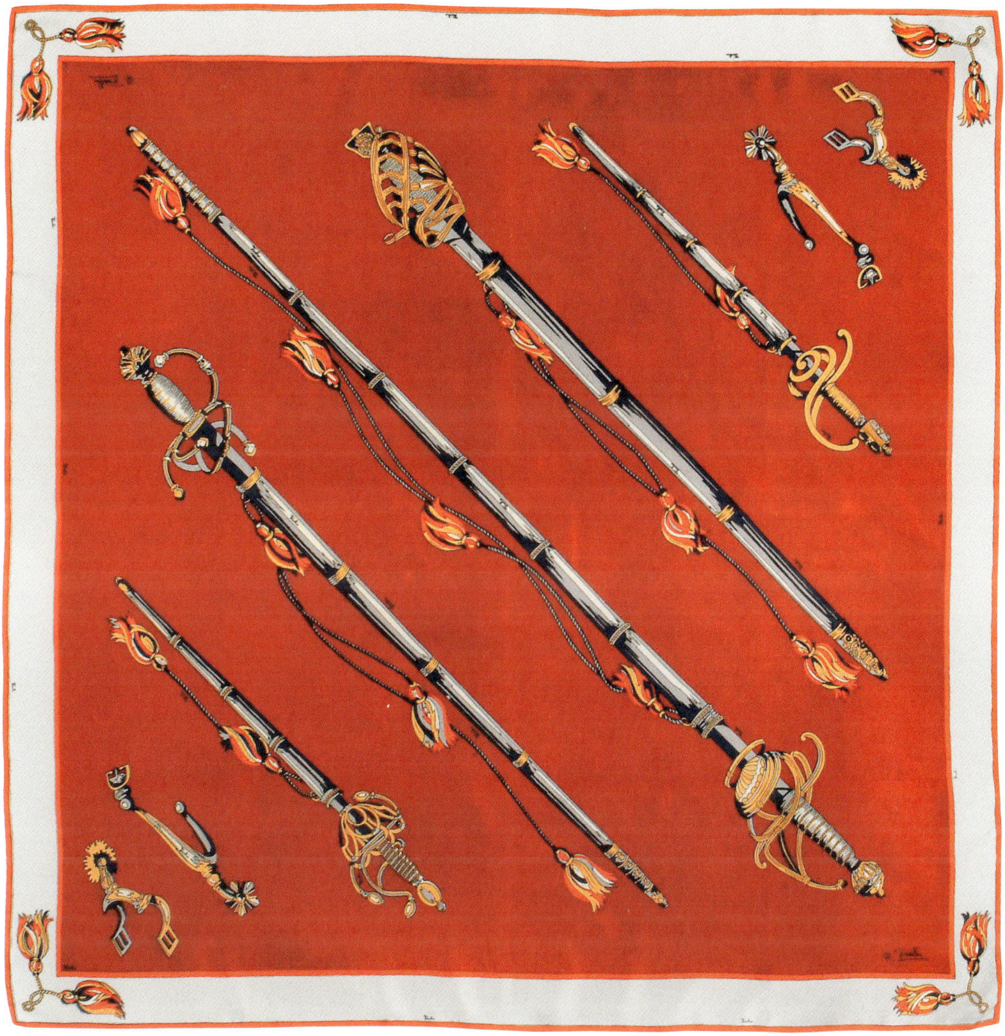

"Spade" scarf, 1980.
Silk twill, 90 x 90 cm.

"It's extraordinary because the heritage is all in one place: Emilio Pucci worked in that palazzo, lived there, the shop was there, the scarves are all framed on the walls, the carpets are there, you open an old closet, and they're lined in turquoise silk. It's stunning. The interesting thing is, the old and the new go so well together—his textiles, with these swirling shapes, and the frescoes—and it's because the new actually came from the old." — Karla Otto

Opposite: Emilio Pucci fits an evening dress created from the "Padiglione" scarf, from the Botticelliana Collection; Palazzo Pucci, Florence, 1957.

"Padiglione" scarf, 1957. Silk twill, 90 x 90 cm. The decorative motif was inspired by the baldachin of the *Madonna del Padiglione* by Botticelli.

> *"He said design had to follow the curve of the body, and for that you need to understand harmony."*
> — Carla Sozzani

Opposite: Loose-fitting evening tunic in multicolored silk jersey. The model is seen on the catwalk in the Sala Bianca Ballroom of Palazzo Pucci, Florence. Fall/Winter 1967 Collection.
Photo: Tenca.

Emilio Pucci checks the final appearance of the models backstage during a fashion show in Stockholm in 1965. Fall/Winter 1965 Collection.
Photo: Torbjorn Earnvall for Kamera Bild.

Emilio Pucci with a model backstage during a fashion show in Stockholm in 1965. Fall/Winter 1965 Collection.
Photo: Torbjorn Earnvall for Kamera Bild.

Opposite: Emilio Pucci dresses a model backstage during a fashion show in Stockholm in 1965. Fall/ Winter 1965 Collection.
Photo: Torbjorn Earnvall for Kamera Bild.

"The Puccis were a very old-fashioned family, and they had always lived in Florence; Emilio had no intention of changing that. He could have—he could have lived in New York, or Paris—but he didn't want to; he loved to be in an old-fashioned place. He had half of Florence employed there. He lived with his traditions: the big Christmas tree, birthday parties. When we were young my mother-in-law lived with us; she was a wonderful lady, very old-fashioned, very Catholic, went to mass every morning, and he loved to come back to that. His strength came from his roots, his background, and this house kept them all. It's like a box, and all the family is inside."

— Cristina Pucci

The Sala Bianca in the Pucci Company's headquarters, Palazzo Pucci. The Sala Bianca was decorated in the early 18th century by the sculptor Giovan Battista Foggini with stuccos and the busts of emperors. Photo: Santi Caleca.

"To be in the palazzo is to be imbued with the spirit of Pucci; there is a great dynamic in the building and it really works to encourage creativity and innovation. It was very important for us to maintain that."

— Bernard Arnault

The Sala Bianca in Palazzo Pucci:
Company's studio. Photos: Santi Caleca.

"As you toured the palazzo, which had been transformed into a riot of color displaying archive pieces from the 1950s alongside art and architecture, some of it dating back to the Renaissance, you realized just how much Pucci influenced 20th-century fashion as we know it, and continues to inspire designers today."

— Diet Prada

Opposite: Palazzo Pucci: 18th-century style table with the scarf "Cornici" chairs, upholstered with paisley "Certaldo" motif; "Menelik" rug. Photo: Santi Caleca.

The "Vivara Room" inside the Emilio Pucci Heritage Hub in Palazzo Pucci features a wallpaper installation with a magnified variation of the historic "Vivara" motif, 2018. Photo: Lapo Quagli.

"It is really a planet unto itself, with the family above the studio. And above the boutique, as in the 17th and 18th centuries, are magnificent frescoes, wood paneling, paintings, furniture, objects, architecture, always opulent but never heavy. I am sensitive to the vibrations of places. I can't work without them. And the ballroom and the Marchese's office were full of them. Everyone felt transported by this unique universe where we also sensed the Marchese's modernity in the mix of the old with the prints."

— Christian Lacroix

Opposite: Laudomia Pucci with a model wearing a dress from the "Collectibles" (Archive reissue) series, 2008. Salone dei Balconi, Palazzo Pucci, Florence.
Photo © Kazutaka Nakamura.

Offices in the Pucci Company headquarters in Palazzo Pucci, Florence, with a rug featuring the "Nastri" motif, and a "Rive Droite" chair by Cappellini.
Photo: Santi Caleca.

Pages 162/163: Pop-up boutique, Emilio Pucci Heritage Hub in Palazzo Pucci, 2018. Photo: Lapo Quagli.

The Odyssey Room, entrance to the Fondazione Emilio Pucci, in Palazzo Pucci: 19th-century frescoes by the painter Henry Wallis, empire banquette upholstered in Vivara silk print. Photo: Lapo Quagli.

Opposite: The video library with the "Up" armchairs, designed by Gaetano Pesce for B&B, upholstered in Emilio Pucci fabrics. Emilio Pucci Heritage Hub in Palazzo Pucci, 2018. Photo: Lapo Quagli.

"La Caccia" scarf, 1959.
Silk twill, 90 x 90 cm. The motif is inspired by the "Stories of Nastagio degli Onesti" by Botticelli.

Opposite: Silk twill cocktail dress featuring the "Caccia" motif. From the Botticelliana Collection, Spring/Summer 1959. Photo: Giulio Guzzoni.

Opposite: Silk twill scarf shirt with the "Primavera" motif, shantung silk trousers. From the Botticelliana Collection, Spring/ Summer 1959.

"Cornici" scarf, 1960s.
Silk twill, 90 x 90 cm.

Emilio Pucci sketches for a wedding dress.

Opposite: Cristina Pucci wears a high-waisted turquoise silk jersey dress; her husband, Emilio Pucci, appears in the background. *Look*, 1960. Photo Robert Randall © Library of Congress, Prints & Photographs Division, Look Magazine Photograph Collection.

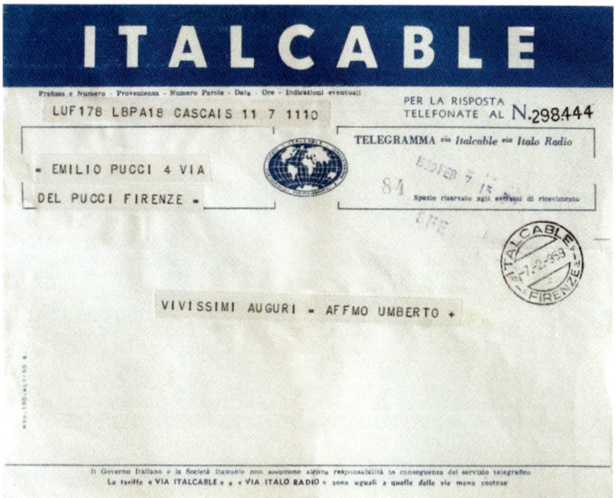
ITALCABLE

Prefisso e Numero - Provenienza - Numero Parole - Data - Ore - Indicazioni eventuali

LUF178 LBPA18 CASCAIS 11 7 1110

PER LA RISPOSTA TELEFONATE AL N. 298444

TELEGRAMMA via Italcable via Italo Radio

Spazio riservato agli estremi di ricevimento

= EMILIO PUCCI 4 VIA
DEL PUCCI FIRENZE =

VIVISSIMI AUGURI = AFFMO UMBERTO +

Il Governo Italiano e la Società Italcable non assumono alcuna responsabilità in conseguenza del servizio telegrafico
Le tariffe « VIA ITALCABLE » e « VIA ITALO RADIO » sono uguali a quelle delle vie meno costose

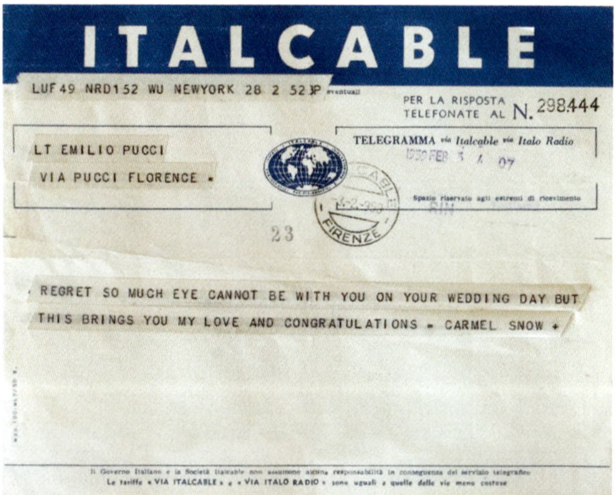
ITALCABLE

LUF49 NRD152 WU NEWYORK 28 2 523P

PER LA RISPOSTA TELEFONATE AL N. 298444

TELEGRAMMA via Italcable via Italo Radio

Spazio riservato agli estremi di ricevimento

LT EMILIO PUCCI
VIA PUCCI FLORENCE =

REGRET SO MUCH EYE CANNOT BE WITH YOU ON YOUR WEDDING DAY BUT
THIS BRINGS YOU MY LOVE AND CONGRATULATIONS = CARMEL SNOW +

Il Governo Italiano e la Società Italcable non assumono alcuna responsabilità in conseguenza del servizio telegrafico
Le tariffe « VIA ITALCABLE » e « VIA ITALO RADIO » sono uguali a quelle delle vie meno costose

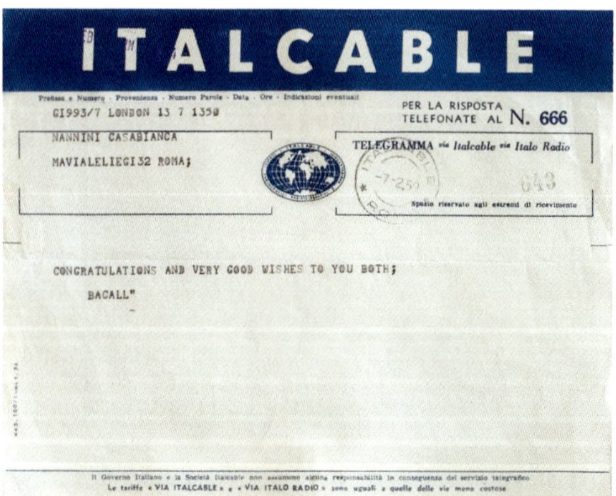
ITALCABLE

Prefisso e Numero - Provenienza - Numero Parole - Data - Ore - Indicazioni eventuali

GI993/7 LONDON 13 7 1350

PER LA RISPOSTA TELEFONATE AL N. 666

TELEGRAMMA via Italcable via Italo Radio

Spazio riservato agli estremi di ricevimento

NANNINI CASABIANCA
MAVIALELIEGI32 ROMA;

CONGRATULATIONS AND VERY GOOD WISHES TO YOU BOTH;
BACALL"

Il Governo Italiano e la Società Italcable non assumono alcuna responsabilità in conseguenza del servizio telegrafico
Le tariffe « VIA ITALCABLE » e « VIA ITALO RADIO » sono uguali a quelle delle vie meno costose

Telegrams sent on the occasion of the marriage Emilio Pucci, Marchese di Barsento, and Cristina Nannini, a baroness in her own right, on February 7, 1959. Courtesy Emilio Pucci Archive, Florence.

"Heartfelt wishes — Umberto" (of Savoy).

"Regret so much not to be with you on your wedding day but this brings you my love and congratulations Carmel Snow."

"Congratulations and very good wishes to you both — Lauren Bacall."

Opposite: Marchese and Marchesa di Barsento, Emilio and Cristina Pucci at the Canzone del Mare in Capri, 1963. *L'Europeo*, 1963. Photo © Duilio Pallottelli/Archivio Rizzoli.

Pages 174/175: Emilio Pucci Heritage Hub in Palazzo Pucci. A display featuring terrycloth and cotton velvet capes in the capsules of the Sala delle Muse. Photo: Lapo Quagli.

Opposite: Fondazione Emilio Pucci, Sala delle Muse Palazzo Pucci, Florence. Silk georgette dress with "Ari" motif, from the Spring/Summer 2009 Collection. Model: Jessica Celeste Michibata. *Glamorous* Japan. Photo © Kazutaka Nakamura.

Printed silk evening dress featuring the "Tra" motif, embroidered all over with Swarovski crystals, 1980s. Photo: Paolo Bacherini.

Silk organza evening dress with straps, printed with the "Fiesole" motif, embroidered all over with Swarovski crystals and sequins, 1980. Photo: Paolo Bacherini.

Opposite: Detail of embroidery with Swarovski crystals and sequins, from the silk organza evening dress printed with the "Fiesole" motif, 1980.

Pages 180/181: Exhibition of embroidered dresses, celebrating the 60th anniversary of the Company in the Fondazione Emilio Pucci, 2007, Palazzo Pucci, Florence.

"R 21" scarf, 1968.
Silk twill, 90 x 90 cm.

Opposite: Villa di Granaiolo, the Pucci family estate: the garden was designed in the 1970s by the architect Gae Aulenti. *House and Garden*, 1971.
Photo de Benedetti/© Condé Nast.

"The country place was the same; it had been in the family since the 15th century. Emilio inherited it when an uncle died, and he wanted to live in it right away, but there was no central heating, very old bathrooms, and we had to do it all up. He said to me, 'just do a few rooms, so we can have a shooting party,' but he knew that once you do a few rooms, you need to do them all. It took almost three years, but he loved it there."

— Cristina Pucci

The Living Wardrobe

The House of Pucci didn't originate in an art school, it came from a life school, and in the beginning the imperative was simple: to get rid of the constrictive, subdued uniform of sport and allow the exuberance of schussing at high speed down a slope to have sartorial expression. There were no complicated philosophical underpinnings to the garments, just a straightforward desire to solve a problem: to take the old-fashioned and render it contemporary, and useful. Remember, the first Pucci garment was a Reed ski team uniform, and today one of the most successful collaborations has been with Rossignol. This is partly why Pucci was so easy to wear and so easy to like: the women and men who saw the pieces immediately recognized how they could, and can, fit into their lives. Like most breakthroughs, in retrospect it seems so obvious—color and stretch—but it actually was the fruit of both technological effort and great chutzpah. To change a paradigm is a shocking thing.

Ski suit Emilio Pucci/ Rossignol Collection, "Elettra" motif.
Winter 2007 Collection.
Art direction: Ezra Petronio.
Photo © Magnus Unnar.

N
NE
E
SE
S
SO
O
NO
Emilio

CERVINIA

"Emilio was very sporty in the beginning, and doing his resort look, with lots of trousers and shirts. At the time in Italy, no one understood sportswear, but because he had been in America and because it was part of his identity, he did. He understood that it wasn't just him that wanted to move like that and have that freedom, but that women wanted to be on the street, that they wanted to change, and they wanted to change on the beach, or skiing."

— Cristina Pucci

Pages 186/187: Detail of "Cervinia" scarf, 1952. Silk twill, 89 x 89 cm.

Opposite: Ski suit with white cable-knit wool sweater and white elasticized wool gabardine trousers. Fall/Winter 1957 Collection. Photo: Relang, Munich.

Two Pucci ski outfits; one with striped jacket, trousers and sweater, the other with printed velvet jacket, elasticized wool gabardine trousers and sweater with diagonal stripes. *Vogue* USA, November 1966. Photo: William Klein, Vogue © Condé Nast.

Opposite top to bottom: Poppi de Salis wears a ski suit with a warm wool shirt and wool gabardine "streamliners" ski pants, 1947. Photo © Toni Frissell/*Harper's Bazaar.*

Poppi de Salis wears a hand-knitted wool vest and wool gabardine ski pants, Zermatt, 1947. Photo © Toni Frissell/*Harper's Bazaar.*

Above: Invitation for the presentation of the Fall/Winter 2008 Collection reproduced on the cover of *Sports Illustrated*, 1969. Waterproof cotton velvet ski jacket and elasticized fabric trousers; Cortina d'Ampezzo, November 1969. Photo © Ernst Haas/*Sports Illustrated.*

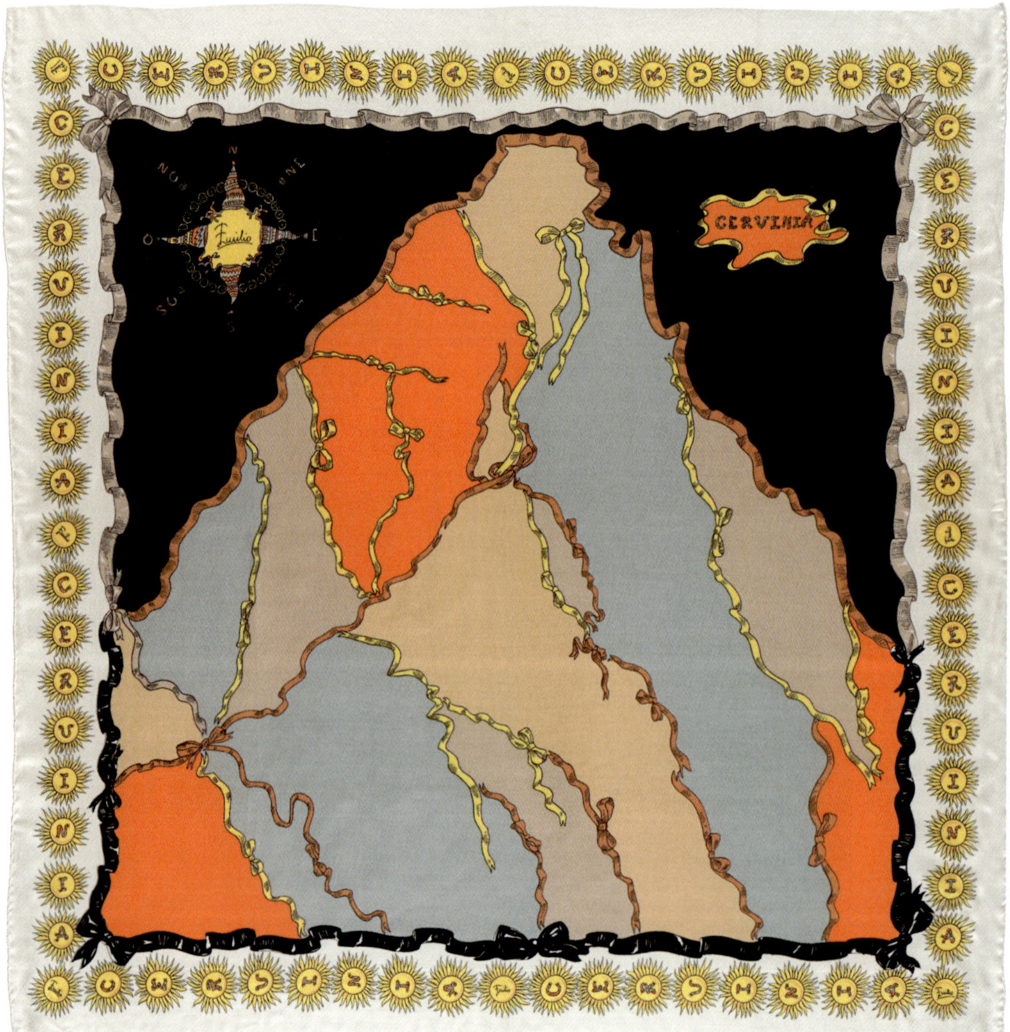

"Cervinia" scarf, 1952.
Silk twill, 89 x 89 cm.

Opposite: Emilio Pucci and Mary Palen in Zermatt, 1949.

"Skiing was really the Marchese's passion and reason for being. Although what was ultra-new or avant-garde in the 1950s and '60s had become classic and normal in 2000, there was no question that sport still needed a style, and that was what the Marchese had launched. So when I joined we made the decision to bring it back, and put a lot of emphasis on ski collections."

— Christian Lacroix

"Corviglia Club" limited edition scarf, created for the Corviglia Club in St. Moritz, 1950s. Silk twill, 90 x 90 cm.

"Alpi" scarf. Fall/Winter 2008/09
Collection. Silk twill, 90 x 90 cm.

Drawing for "Abetone" scarf, 1957. China ink and tempera on paper, 79 x 79 cm.

Opposite: Emilio Pucci fastens a ski for Poppi de Salis, who wears a Pucci ski outfit: wool shirt with hood buttoned on the neck, wool gabardine "streamliners" trousers; Zermatt, 1947. *Harper's Bazaar*, December 1948. Photo: Toni Frissel. Courtesy Emilio Pucci Archive, Florence.

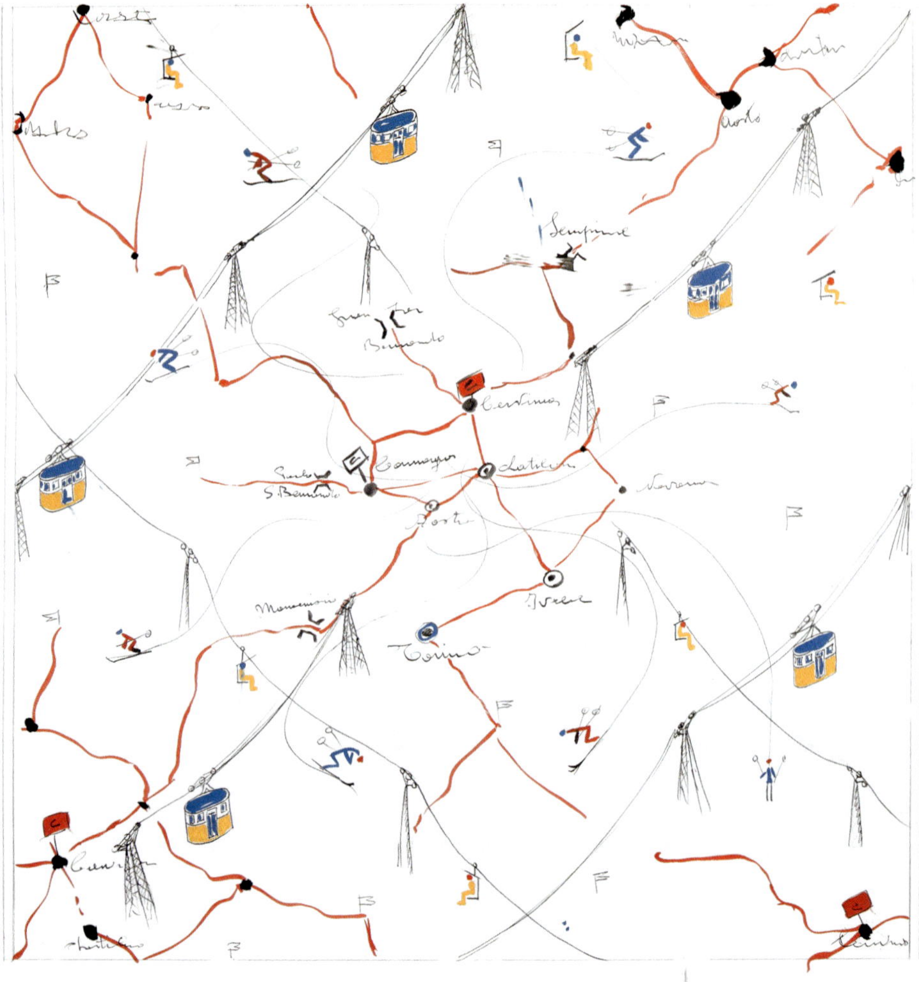

"Albergo Cervinia II" drawing, 1956.
Pencil, tempera and china ink on paper,
96 x 100 cm.

Opposite: Drawing for "Sestriere"
scarf. Marker on paper, 94 x 92 cm.

C. GOLF SESTRIERE
CHIESA DI S. EDOARDO
MONTE FRAITEVE
MONTE BANCHETTA
BORGATA SESTRIERE
SKI LIFT BORGATA - SESTRIERE
MONTE SISES
LA SERENELLA
ALBERGO TORRE
DIANA SPORT
ALBERGO SESTRIERE
FUNIVIA FRAITEVE
CASA DEL COMUNE
Maria Cristina
S. EDOARDO
TELEFONO - POSTA
NEGOZI
SCUOLA NAZ. DI SCI
GENZIANELLA - TEA ROOM
CINEMATOGRAFO
RISTORANTE TURISTICO
APPARTAMENTI
CENTRALE ELETTRICA
BAR
GRANDE ALBERGO DUCHI D'AOSTA
CAMPO DI PATTINAGGIO
SKI LIFT MONTE SISES
FONTANA NAPOLEONICA
SESTRIERE
GRANDE ALBERGO PRINCIPI DI PIEMONTE
GOLF 18 BUCHE
CLASSE CANNONI
CLASSE I
SCUOLA NAZIONALE DI SCI
PARTICOLARI DEL PORTALE CENTRALE DI SANT' EDOARDO

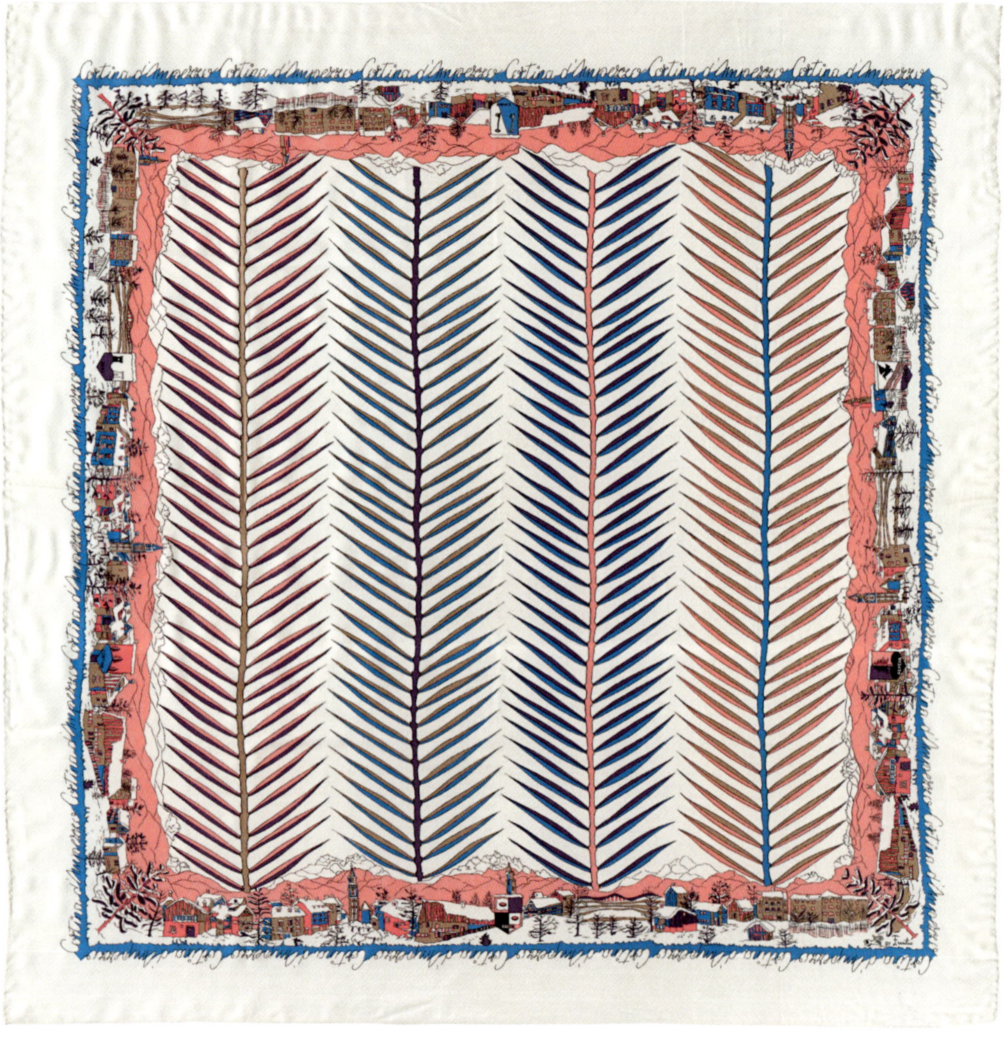

"Cortina d'Ampezzo" scarf, 1957.
Silk twill, 90 x 90 cm.

"Bouquet" scarf, 1967.
Silk twill, 90 x 90 cm.

Pages 202/203: Detail of "Gioielli del Mare" scarf, 1950s. Silk twill, 90 x 90 cm.

Drawing for "Finmare" special edition scarf. Tempera on paper, 49 x 53 cm.

"Gaviota IV" special edition scarf,
designed for Motor Yacht *Gaviota IV*.
Silk twill, 70 x 70 cm.

"He understood the woman he was dressing, because the life she lived was also his life: in the winter, St. Moritz; in the summer, Capri. He designed clothes for what he believed in, and you could feel that integrity. It was very appealing."

— Polly Mellen

Opposite: Multicolored stripes poncho beach-robe in cotton popeline, conical straw hat, Capri. Spring/Summer 1954 Collection.

"Creole" special edition scarf, designed for Stavros Niarchos's yacht *Creole*, 1954. Silk twill, 65 x 65 cm.

Top: Multicolored striped poncho beach-robe in cotton popeline, colored straw hat, Capri. Spring/ Summer 1954 Collection. Photo: Lee Thody.

Bottom: Two-colored striped poncho beach-robe in cotton popeline, straw hat, Capri. Spring/Summer 1954 Collection. Photo: Lee Thody.

Opposite: "Pesci" scarf, 1969. Silk twill, 90 x 90 cm.

"It's a living brand, and to be a part of that you have to participate in the values it represents. This really spoke to me as both a man and a designer: I love to ski, and I want to end my days on a beach. I love freedom; I left home at thirteen. I've always been the black sheep of my family, and I felt I had this in common with the house."

— Peter Dundas

"Because of the focus on the sun and sea and your skin, it had this incredible magnetism. Men went crazy over those clothes on a woman. The way those clothes draped on the body and clung to you!"

— Polly Mellen

Veruschka poses on the "Pink Rocks" of Fazenda Tangua, Brazil, wearing a printed cotton bikini with the "Navaho" scarf motif, with matching sarong-skirt. Spring/Summer 1965 Collection. Photo © Henry Clarke/ Condé Nast Collection/Getty Images.

"Ombrelloni" drawing. China ink and watercolor on board, 1958.

Opposite: Embroidered silk shirt featuring the "Nisida" motif. Spring/Summer 2018 Collection. Model: Edmée di Robilant. Elle Brazil, March 2018. Photo © Leo Faria/ELLE Brazil.

"Mar dei Sargassi" scarf, 1950s. Silk twill, 90 x 90 cm.

Pages 216–219: "Porti di mare" series of scarves, late 1950s. Silk jersey, 60 x 60 cm.

"Porto Santo Stefano"

"Porto Azzurro"

"Porto Ercole"

"Portofino"

Pages 220/221: Cotton jersey trousers and silk top with the "Ellisse" motif. Spring/Summer 2002 Collection. *Vogue* Australia, 2002.
Photo © Torkil Gudnason.

Worldly Inspiration

"[Pucci] has returned from the vast continent with a burning sense of its dangerous beauty…the marvelous lines breathe the power of the sun and shield against its excesses—enveloping the body in sun-wild freedom and seduction." So wrote American *Vogue* of Pucci's original Africa-inspired collection, full of capes and silk-chiffon pajamas. One of the many trips that informed his collections, the African odyssey not only expanded Pucci's color palette, but also produced entirely new illustrations that reflected everything from the waves of Lake Tanganyika to the sun setting over the veldt. As much as any actual place, however, the trips reflected the identity of the brand as truly global, an identity that derived from the Marchese's own perception of himself as a citizen of the world, wherever he was—America or Switzerland, Bali or Russia. His was a vision rooted in Italy but appreciative of other cultures and countries, and this has expanded over the years as his creative successors, who grew up in different countries, brought their own cultures to the house. In a sense, Pucci was one of the first brands to have an international vision that was not simply about how you could sell a design label around the world (although it did just that), but also about the future interconnectedness of all countries. And the vision was expressed, as always, in cloth.

Samantha Jones, in the Lake Palace in Udaipur, Rajasthan, India, wears a hooded silk jersey mini dress in the "Foglie" panel motif. Spring/Summer 1967 Collection. Photo © Henry Clarke/ Condé Nast Collection/Getty Images.

"He told me a story about the Africa Collection, and how he did a long color study there that involved 24 hours in the same place next to a lake, in a forest. The result was a collection made of shades of the different hours of the day. He said, 'You have to take a drawing, use different elements together and then you color them: it is a ping-pong of colors.'"

— Carla Sozzani

Pages 224/225: "The water carriers" drawing, 1963. China ink and tempera on paper, 52.8 x 48 cm.

Opposite: "Niger" panel, 1964. Silk crêpe, 90 x 130 cm.

"Naga" scarf, 1964. Silk twill, 90 x 90 cm.

Opposite: Printed silk jersey evening dress in the "Foglie" motif, with bodice embroidered with beads and Swarovski crystals, earrings and gem-encrusted sandals by Coppola e Toppo. Spring/Summer 1967 Collection. Photo: Renzo Pavanello.

"Foglie" panel, 1967.
Silk twill, 90 x 130 cm.

"When he traveled, he only ever wanted to eat his favorite yogurts and some apples. He was a little odd that way, but it was right for him."

— Hubert de Givenchy

"Naiwasha" scarf, 1977.
Silk twill, 90 x 90 cm.

Opposite: Silk organza dress fully encrusted with Swarovski crystals in the "Naiwasha" scarf motif.

"Congo" scarf, 1967.
Silk twill, 90 x 90 cm.

"Arcieri" scarf, 1977.
Silk twill, 90 x 90 cm.

“Angoli” scarf, 1967.
Silk twill, 90 x 90 cm.

"Quadrifoglio" scarf, 1971.
Cotton gabardine, 90 x 90 cm.

"He was always moving: intellectually, physically."

— Cristina Pucci

"Mala-Mala" scarf, 1970
Silk twill, 90 x 90 cm.

Opposite: Printed Lycra leggings in the "Mala-Mala" scarf motif, Spring/Summer 2003/04 Collection. *Elle France 3000*, June 2003.
Photo © Friedemann Hauss/Elle/Scoop.

"Bwana" scarf, 1960s.
Silk twill, 66 x 66 cm.

"Nirvana Sun" panel,
silk georgette, 120 x 120 cm.

Opposite: Printed silk crêpe cocktail dress in the "Galloni" panel motif, oriental skirt, earrings and sandals. Spring/Summer 1966 Collection.
Photo: Centro internazionale Arti e costume Palazzo Grassi, Venice.

Detail of the drawing for the "Mikonos" panel, 1974. Marker on paper, 133 x 151 cm.

"The truth is, every part of the world offers a mind-boggling source of inspiration and it is an impossibility not to draw from one's surroundings—everywhere."

— Peter Dundas

Opposite: "Stella" scarf, 1967.
Silk twill, 90 x 90 cm.

Silk chiffon embroidered dress in the "Stella" motif. Spring/Summer 2004 Collection. *Squint*, May 2004.
Photo © Marc Philbert.

Simone D'Aillencourt in the Lake Palace in Udaipur, Rajasthan, India, wears a silk crêpe catsuit; the trouser hems are embroidered with Swarovski crystals and a wide poncho in printed silk chiffon is in the "Lance" motif. Photo © Henry Clarke/Condé Nast Collection/Getty Images.

Pages 246/247: Python and suede jacket; cotton ottoman skirt and silk jersey tunic in the "Sundial" motif. Spring/Summer 2008 Collection. Palazzo Gangi, Palermo, Italy. Photo © Juergen Teller.

"Idolo" scarf, 1960.
Silk twill, 90 x 90 cm.

"Arazzo" scarf, 1963.
Silk twill, 90 x 90 cm.

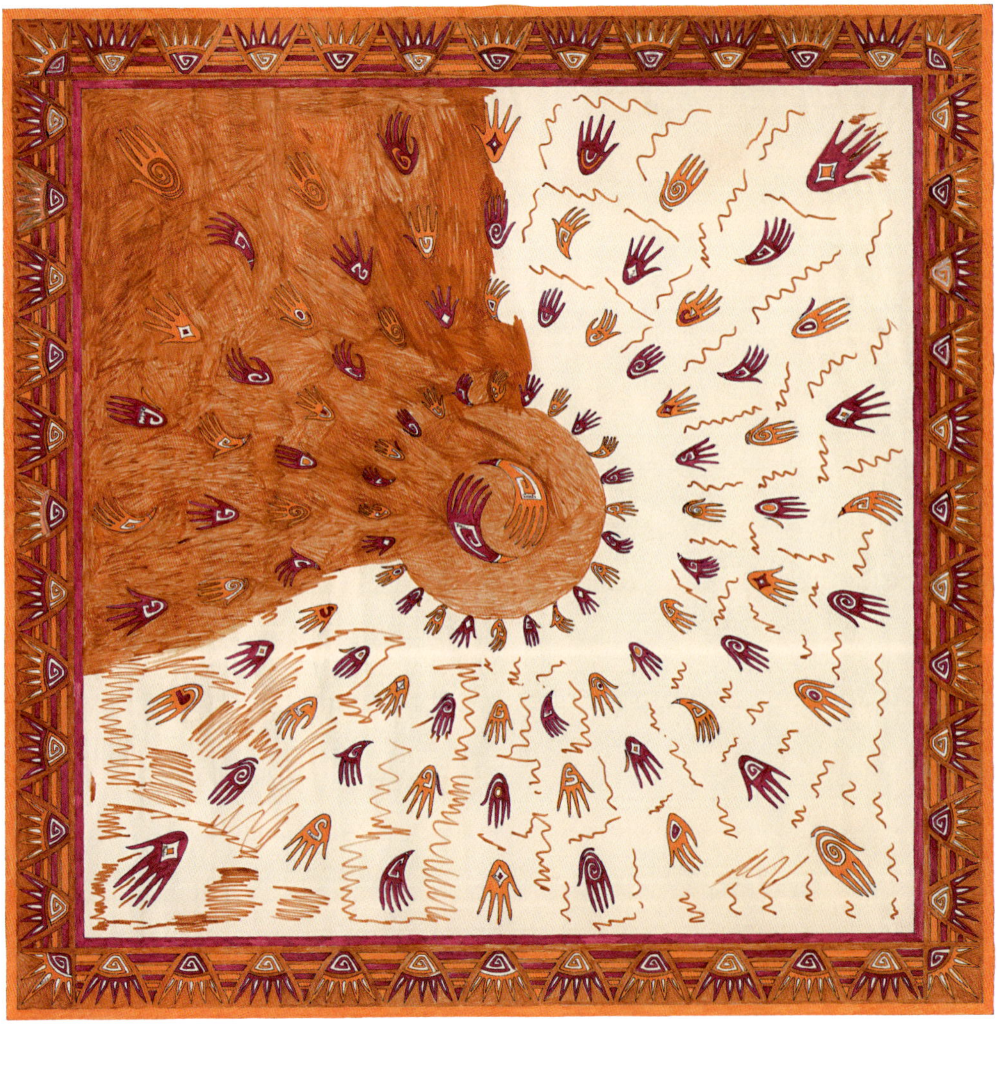

Drawing for the "Manine" scarf, 1977. Marker on paper, 72 x 74 cm.

Opposite: Printed cotton tunic in the "Azteco" motif, straw hat. Spring/Summer 1952 Collection.

"Manine" scarf, 1977.
Cotton batiste, 65 x 65 cm.

"Piedini" scarf, 1977.
Cotton batiste 65 x 65 cm.

"Bermuda's Gombey Dance" scarf, 1954. Silk twill, 90 x 90 cm.

"Specchi" scarf, 1961.
Silk twill, 90 x 90 cm.

"Ladeco" scarf, 1970s.
Silk twill, 90 x 90 cm.

"Ruota" scarf, 1970.
Silk twill, 90 x 90 cm.

Opposite: "Anonimo" drawing, 1962. Watercolor and tempera on paper, 100 x 120 cm.

"Occhiate" panel, 1966. Silk twill, 80 x 120 cm.

Opposite: Printed silk velvet suit in the "Sarna" panel motif; short-sleeved bolero and long, straight skirt, with pink silk jersey top. Fall/Winter 1963 Collection. *Harper's Bazaar*, December 1963. Photo © Melvin Sokolsky.

"Manis" panel, 1963.
Silk jersey, 90 x 120 cm.

"What's interesting is, if you look at the prints, you can see he entered into every landscape he saw without ever vulgarizing himself."

— Christian Lacroix

Opposite: "Spring" panel, 1966. Silk twill, 90 x 130 cm.

Printed silk chiffon dress in the "Iside" panel motif, worn over a Lycra jumpsuit with matching print. Spring/Summer 1966 Collection. Model: Susan Murray. Photo © Henry Clarke/Condé Nast Collection/Getty Images.

Page 264: Drawing for "Tulipani" panel, 1965. Colored pencil, marker, white tempera, ink on paper, 90 x 130 cm.

Page 265: Detail of drawing for "Paisly" panel, 1967. Colored pencil, marker, white tempera, ink on paper, 90 x 120 cm.

Printed silk jersey evening dress in the "Paisly" panel motif; Machu Picchu, Peru. Spring/Summer 1966 Collection.

Palazzo pajamas: silk twill jacket and flared trousers in the "Arabesco" panel motif. Spring/Summer 1966 Collection.

Opposite: Sarong dress worn over printed silk twill trousers in the "Concentrico" scarf motif, sandals. Spring/Summer 1966 Collection. Model: Iko. Photo: Lumachi.

"Concentrico" scarf, 1966. Silk twill, 90 x 90 cm.

"Bangkok" panel, 1967.
Silk georgette, 90 x 140 cm.

Opposite: Aristotle Onassis and his wife Jackie; Jackie wears a printed silk jersey mini dress in the "Bangkok" panel motif. Capri 1967. Courtesy Emilio Pucci Archive, Florence.

Page 274: Printed silk organza cocktail tunic mini dress in the "Concentrico" scarf motif, Helanca leggings with matching print, both embroidered, earrings by Coppola e Toppo for Emilio Pucci. Spring/Summer 1966 Collection. Photo: Lumachi.

Page 275: Cocktail outfit with a printed twill silk scarf mini dress in the "Concentrico" motif over Helanca leggings in the same print and matching shoes. Spring/Summer 1966 Collection. Model: Iko. Photo: Lumachi.

"Garuda" scarf, 1963.
Silk twill, 90 x 90 cm.

"Evoluzioni" scarf, 1966.
Silk twill, 90 x 90 cm.

"Cactus" scarf, 1997.
Silk twill, 90 x 90 cm.

"Fiamma" scarf, 1974.
Silk twill, 90 x 90 cm.

"Manila" scarf, 1974.
Silk twill, 90 x 90 cm.

"Cactus" scarf, 1967.
Silk twill, 90 x 90 cm.

Opposite: Jessica Celeste Michibata on the stone staircase of the roof terrace of Palazzo Pucci wears a printed silk mini dress in the "Miri Grande" motif, Spring/Summer 2009 Collection. *Glamorous* Japan, November 2008. Photo © Kazutaka Nakamura.

"Miri Grande" scarf, 2008. Silk organza, 140 x 140 cm.

"He liked to talk about his 1957 Russian collection, where there were 197 colors on the runway. Each place had its own palette, and he said each print had its own personality." — Carla Sozzani

Drawing for "Alabarde" scarf, 1970.
Tempera, pencil and ink on paper,
90 x 90 cm.

"Ranuncoli" drawing, 1971. Colored pencil, marker, white tempera, ink on paper, 90 x 90 cm.

"Ranuncoli" scarf, 1971.
Silk twill, 90 x 90 cm.

"Westinghouse" scarf, 1970s.
Cotton batiste, 90 x 90 cm.

Top: "Fantasia 1" scarf, 1970.
Cotton batiste, 65 x 65 cm.

Bottom: "Westinghouse" scarf,
1970s. Cotton batiste, 90 x 90 cm.

Right: Hooded printed
cotton velveteen cape dress in
the "Evoluzioni" scarf motif.
Spring/Summer 1966 Collection.
Photo: Alessandro Mossotti.

Long, one-tone silk jersey dress with embroidered bodice. Detail of the heart-shaped neckline of the bodice and the Swarovski crystal-encrusted straps in subtle nuances of color. Fall/Winter 1974 Collection.
Pages 290–301 Photos: Paolo Bacherini.

Opposite: Evening outfit: long, one-tone silk jersey dress with embroidered bodice, silk organza jacket in the "Dentelle" motif, embroidered all over with Swarovski crystals. Fall/Winter 1974 Collection.

Palazzo pajamas with pointed neckline embroidered with Swarovski crystals, loose silk chiffon harem pants in the "Vivara" motif, 1967.

Palazzo pajamas in silk georgette with "Occhi" motif: bodice with straps and edges embroidered all over with Swarovski crystals, 1970s.

Palazzo pajamas with short top and low-waisted oriental skirt in silk organza printed in the "Chianti" motif, embroidered on the neckline and on the edges with Swarovski crystals. Spring/Summer 1972 Collection.

Palazzo pajamas in printed silk crêpe with the "Cometa" motif; sarong skirt with embroidered edges and fringes, side slit revealing one-legged trousers; triangle shaped top and brassiere embroidered all over with Swarovski crystals. Spring/Summer 1970 Collection.

Palazzo pajamas with sleeveless top and silk organza sarong skirt, printed in the "Grate di bronzo" motif, embroidered all over with Swarovski crystals. Fall/Winter 1966 Collection.

Evening dress with straps and pointed edge in silk organza with the "Giacinti" motif, embroidered with sequins and Swarovski crystals. Spring/Summer 1982 Collection.

Two-piece evening dress in silk chiffon printed in the "Dischi" motif: fluid line sleeveless dress cut on the bias, bra top with crystal clasp, long puff sleeves with cuffs embroidered with Swarovski crystals. Spring/Summer 1967 Collection.

Palazzo pajamas in printed silk organza with the "Ciclamini" motif, harem pants, edges and neckline embroidered with Swarovski crystals, 1973.

Evening dress in printed silk organza with the "Centrino" motif: tight-fitting dress with straps and side slit revealing one-legged trousers. Spring/Summer 1982 Collection.

Opposite: Detail of the Swarovski crystal embroidery on the evening dress with the "Centrino" motif. Spring/Summer 1982 Collection.

Opposite: Palazzo pajamas with printed silk turban embroidered with Swarovski crystals, from the Fall/Winter 1969 Collection. Photo: Gian Paolo Barbieri, courtesy of Fondazione Gian Paolo Barbieri ETS, © Giada Barbieri.

Detail of the drawing for the "Farfalla" scarf, 1965. Marker, crayon and china ink on paper, 93 x 103 cm.

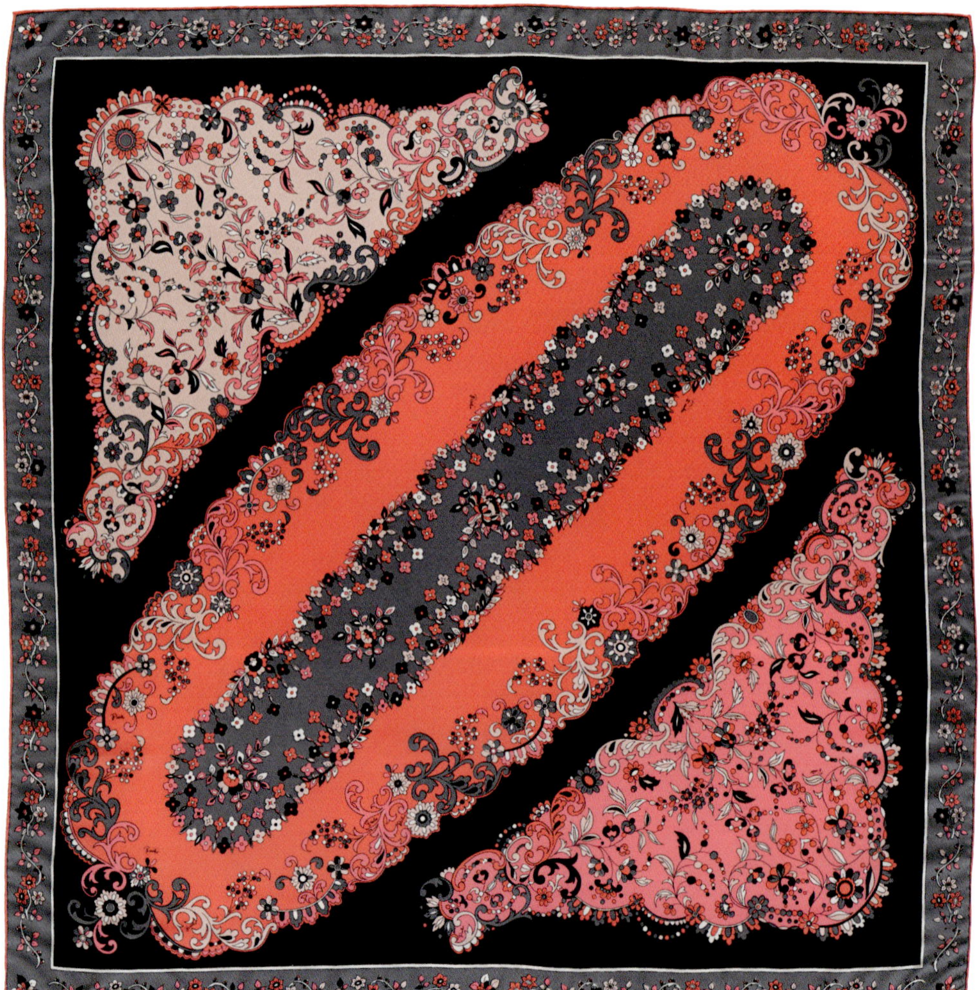

"Fantasia" scarf, 1965.
Silk twill, 90 x 90 cm.

"Cupola" scarf, 1972.
Silk twill, 90 x 90 cm.

Mirella Petteni Haggiag wears printed silk jersey palazzo pajamas in the "Minaret" motif with matching silk turban. Spring/Summer 1967 Collection. Photo: Gian Paolo Barbieri, courtesy of Fondazione Gian Paolo Barbieri ETS, © Giada Barbieri.

"For him prints were rhythm and movement, and in prints he expressed a message of contagious happiness."

— Laudomia Pucci

"Tulipani" scarf, 1970.
Silk twill, 90 x 90 cm.

Opposite: Actress Goya Toledo wears a long dress in silk featuring the "Porticato" motif. Pre Fall 2012 Collection. *Elle* Spain, September 2012. Photo © Bernardo Doral/ELLE Spain.

Pages 310/311: Long dress in black silk. Spring/Summer 2012 Collection. Model: Naty Chabanenko. Stylist: Ivana Spernicelli. *Marie Claire* Italy, April 2012. Photo © Elina Kechicheva/ Marie Claire Italia.

Laced top and long skirt. Spring/ Summer 2012 Collection. Model: Bianca Balti. *Vogue* Japan, June 2012. Photo © Giampaolo Sgura.

Opposite: Long dress embroidered with golden thread, featuring the "Scorpio" motif. Fall/Winter 2015/16 Collection. *Harper's Bazaar* China, December 2015. Model: Liu Wen. Photo © Sun Jun/Harper's Bazaar China.

Travels in Art

On the walls of the Pucci palazzo are many gold frames, and in the frames are scarves—although that word doesn't do them justice. Stretched like a canvas and shown as a pure design, they clearly deserve their display, yet Emilio Pucci always refuted the idea that he was an artist. Whether or not you choose to bestow upon him that title, however (and many did), or prefer to call him an illustrator, or a doodler, or any of the other words that have been used to describe the house's relationship with pattern, there can be no doubt that the art world and the Pucci world are very closely linked; the first inspired the second, and continues to do so. Indeed, when it was decided that the creative reins were to be passed to Christian Lacroix, one of the reasons oft-cited was Lacroix's credentials as a "colorist," while his successor Matthew Williamson's affiliations to the ethos of the house partly derive from his background as a textile designer. It is not just pattern that demonstrates the give-and-take between art and artisan, however—indeed, pattern is only a part of the whole—but, more than pattern, the colors employed in the whole, whether they be color combinations or single shades. As Clarice Pecori Giraldi says, "The clothes produce the same emotions in people that works of art do; your reaction to them is visceral, not intellectual."

Stella Tennant wears a printed silk jersey evening dress with the "Riviera" motif, white resin bracelets; Villa Tritone, Sorrento, Italy. Spring/Summer 2009 Collection. Photo © Juergen Teller.

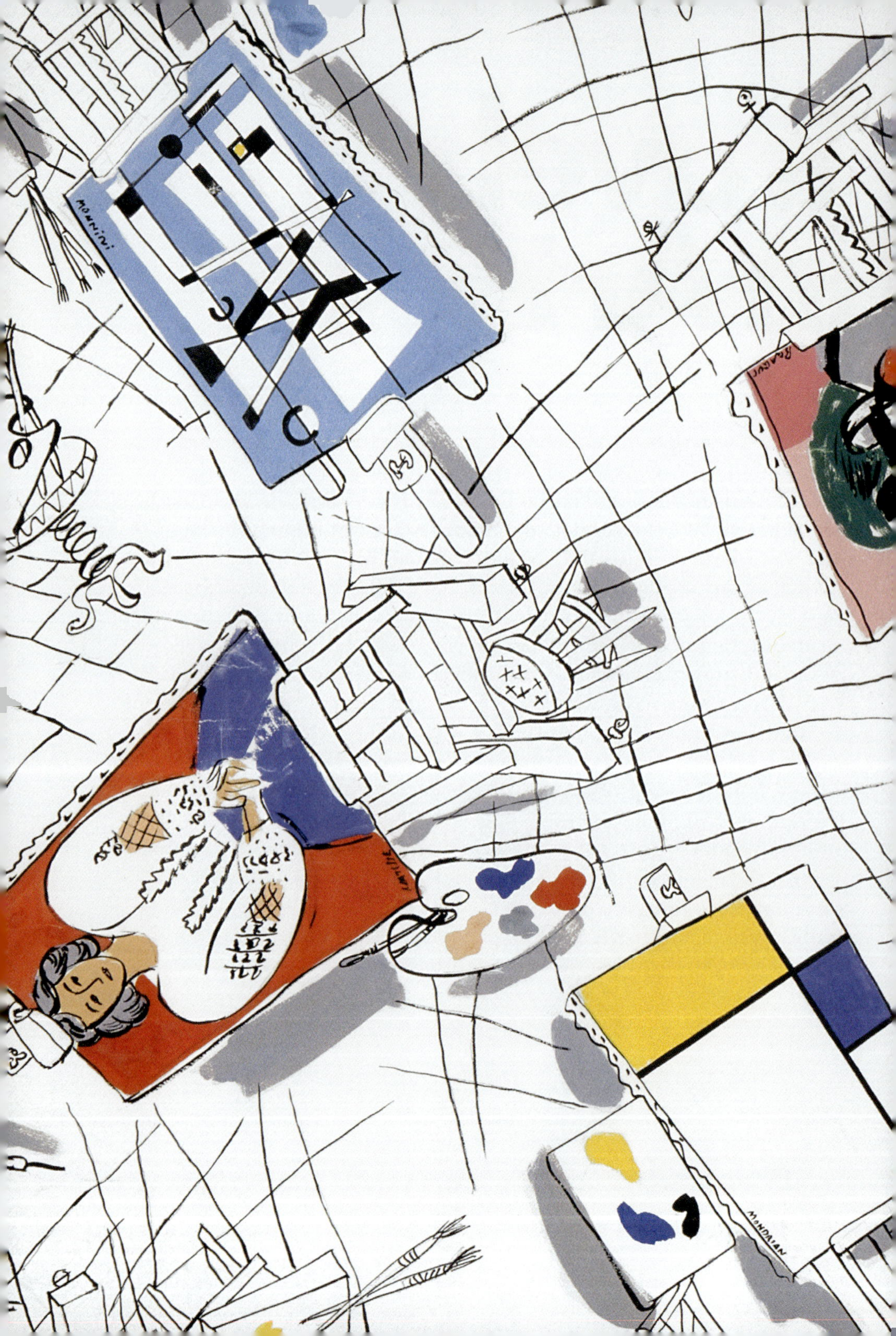

MIRÓ

Pages 316/317: Detail of the drawing "Ateliers," 1957. Pencil and watercolor, 135 x 63 cm.

Drawing for the "Lilium" panel. Pencil on paper, 133 x 133 cm.

"Libellula" scarf, 1980.
Silk crêpe, 90 x 90 cm.

Salvador Dalí and his wife Gala in Paris, watching a model on the catwalk wearing a printed silk jersey dress, 1963.

"Ebes" scarf, 1983.
Silk crêpe, 90 x 90 cm.

"Airone" scarf, 1962.
Silk twill, 90 x 90 cm.

"He admitted that his concept of art is close to the art concept of the Renaissance. He didn't much like modern art."

— Carla Sozzani

Drawing for the "Ventola" scarf. Pencil and china ink on paper, 91 x 96 cm.

Opposite: "Zebrato" dress: cotton sateen mini dress with two-tone poncho collar buttoned on the shoulder. Spring/Summer 1963 Collection. Photo: Leombruno — Bodi.

"We went to New York City once, and I knew nothing about modern art, but he would be out working all day and I would go to galleries, such as Leo Castelli, and when he came home at night I would say, 'I have seen the most amazing thing!' which was all the Pop art, and he would say, 'You cannot like that,' but I wanted to buy it, and then he would say, 'ridiculous, they are awful.' But every night I was talking about it, and finally he said, 'Okay, if you like it so much, I will do it, and do it better,' and he started scratching. Those psychedelic prints went on for a long time."

— Cristina Pucci

Beatriz Milhazes, *Beleza Pura*, 2006.

Opposite: Detail of "Occhi" drawing, 1970s. Pencil on paper, 91 x 102 cm.

Silk jersey dress with flared sleeves, in the "Murano" motif. Fall/Winter 2003 Collection. *Glamour* USA, October 2003. Photo © Patric Shaw.

Opposite: Detail of "Bubbles" scarf, 1969. Silk twill, 90 x 90 cm.

Printed cotton popeline shirt in the "Bolle di Capri" motif, 1953.

Opposite top: "Wing" panel. Spring/Summer 2006 Collection. Printed silk twill, 90 x 90 cm.

Opposite bottom: Painting based on a spin art sketch; the explanation on the back says: "This painting was made by Laudomia to celebrate the opening of Damien Hirst Requiem, at the Pinchuk Art Centre." © Damien Hirst. Courtesy of Laudomia Pucci.

"Pompei" drawing, 1984.
Tempera on paper, 88 x 88 cm.

Opposite: Emilio Pucci sculpture decoration, 1971. Photo © Lumachi. Courtesy Emilio Pucci Archive, Florence.

"He said every flower was made for its leaf."
— Carla Sozzani

Veruschka wears a loose barracan in printed silk jersey in the "Onde" motif. Lake Tanganyika, Tanzania. Spring/Summer 1964 Collection.
Photo © Henry Clarke/Condé Nast Collection/Getty Images.

Opposite: Shirt in silk twill featuring the "Shell" motif, Spring/Summer 2018 Collection. Silk blanket worn as a headscarf featuring the "Onde" motif. Model: Emily Liptow. Photo © Armin Morbach/TUSH Magazine.

"Vetrata" scarf, 1966.
Silk twill, 90 x 90 cm.

"I do watercolors myself, and one of the artists I look to most is Turner; I can spend hours looking at his work. Anyway, last December I was at a Turner exhibit in Ferrara, which featured a lot of his watercolors in Naples and Venice, and all the colors you could see in those paintings are the colors you find in Pucci dresses: the dresses with a million shades of blue, or the whites that fade into blue."

— Clarice Pecori Giraldi

"Chiave" scarf, 1971.
Silk twill, 90 x 90 cm.

Opposite: Mini dress in printed silk jersey in the "Cancello" motif, with matching silk twill scarf. Spring/Summer 2009 Collection.

Model: Jessica Celeste Michibata, Palazzo Pucci, Florence.
Photo © Kazutaka Nakamura.

Giuseppe Capogrossi, lithograph, 1958.

Opposite: "Geometrico" print, 1963. Cotton gabardine.

Mel Ramos, *Pucci Pants*, 1966.

Opposite: Emilio Pucci and a model wearing palazzo pajamas in printed silk in the "Torre" motif, with jacket and hat. Fall/Winter 1966 Collection. Photo: Serge Libis.

Detail of "Arcobaleno" drawing, 1980.
Pencil on paper, 92 x 92 cm.

Opposite: Victor Vasarely, *Vonal Prim*, 1975.

Sequined mini dress and high boots. Fall/Winter 2015/16 Collection. Model: Edita Vilkeviciute. *Vogue* Germany, August 2015. Photo © Giampaolo Sgura.

Opposite: Chloé Sevigny wears a vintage Pucci printed silk jersey dress, 1992. Photo © Patrick O'Dell.

TRACKER
SOUTH SWELL
SURE-GRIP International
MOTOBILT
MAUI
Rector
schmitt stix
AIRWALK
Thunder
SLURPEE
Walker SKATEBOARDS
madrid
NO BOZOS!
GULLWING TRUCKS
SURF NA
SIMS
76% UNCL
THE BURNT
PARTY NA
CRUCIAL YOUTH
UNCLE WI SKATEBO
BURTON SNOWBOARDS
SEPTIC DEATH
INDEPENDENT
ULLWING TRUCKS
REFCO
ZOMBIE
TEAM
NOSTIC FRONT
WAR-ZONE

Opposite: Polo shirt and long skirt in printed stretch cotton in the "Quadratini" motif. Fall/Winter 1997 Collection. Photo: Lucio Gelsi.

Clockwise from top left:
"Quadratini" scarf, 1968.
Silk crêpe, 90 x 90 cm.

"Maremma" scarf, 1981.
Silk crêpe, 90 x 90 cm.

"Giardino" scarf, 1968.
Silk twill, 90 x 90 cm.

Opposite: Claudia Schiffer wears a long draped dress in silk jersey featuring the "Quadratini" motif. Fall/Winter 2017/18 Collection. *Harper's Bazaar* Russia, November 2017.
Photo © Agata Pospieszynska/Harper's Bazaar Russia.

"Moiré" scarf, 1970.
Silk twill, 90 x 90 cm.

Pages 352/353: Printed silk twill dress in the "Moiré" motif, with colored mink shrug, Emilio Pucci sandals. Fall/Winter 2004/05 Collection. *Vogue* Germany, August 2004.
Photo © Javier Vallhonrat.

"He always said nothing natural could ever clash."

— Laudomia Pucci

"Galli" drawing, 1970. Pencil and tempera on paper, 100 x 110 cm.

Above: "Trifoglio" scarf, 1970. Silk twill, 90 x 130 cm.

Left: Fortunato Depero, *Ritmi veneziani*, small tapestry made in 1921/23.

Printed silk dress in the "Collane" panel motif with velvet bodice and velvet jacket lined in matching silk twill. Palazzo Pucci, Florence. Fall/Winter 2004/05 Collection. *Vogue* Russia, August 2004. Photo © Fabio Pettinari.

Opposite: "Collane" panel, 1971. Silk twill, 170 x 180 cm.

"Pucci really introduced an entire spectrum of color to a war-rationed continent, and as a result I think made as much of an impact on the postwar fashion world as Christian Dior."

— Andrew Bolton

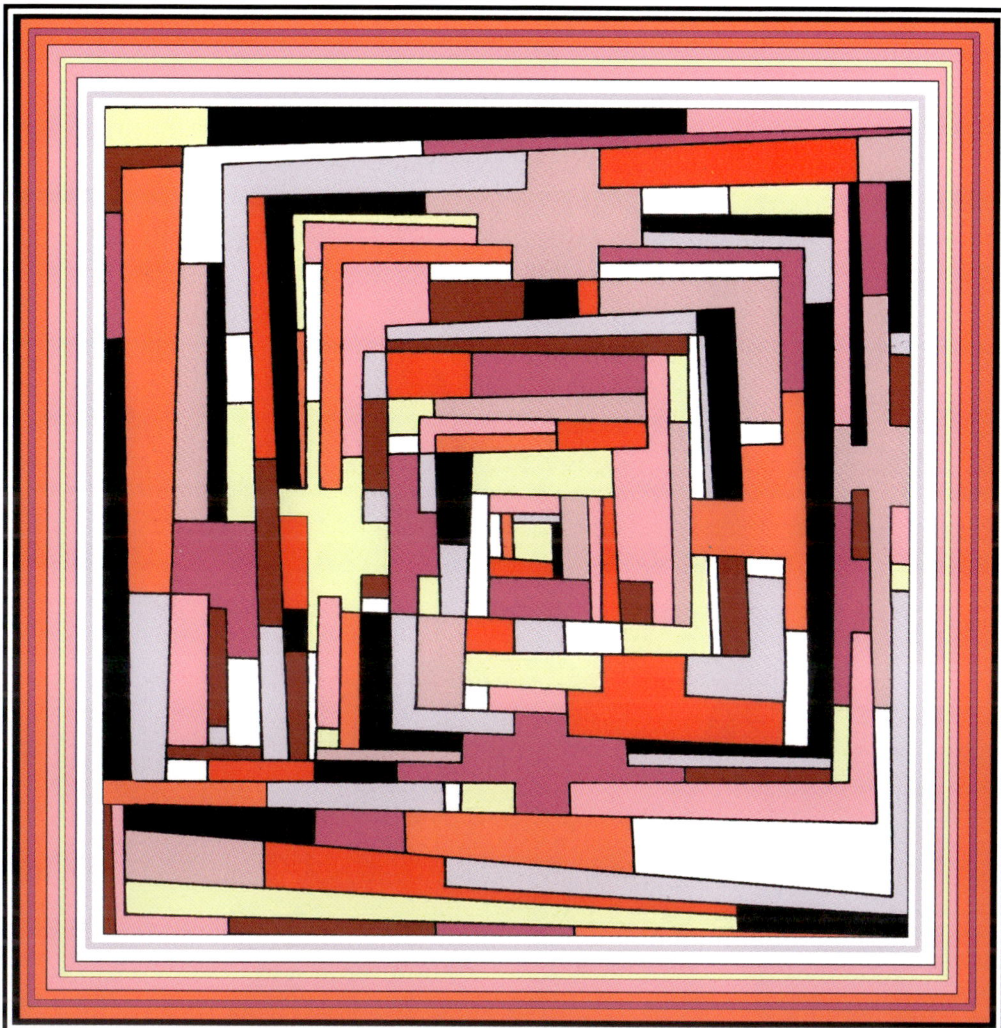

Opposite: Drawing for a scarf.
Tempera on paper, 94 x 94 cm.
Never went into production.

"Zigurat" scarf, 2001.
Silk twill, 90 x 90 cm.

"Fantasia" scarf, 1970.
Silk twill, 90 x 90 cm.

"Cuori" scarf, 2002.
Silk twill, 90 x 90 cm.

"Mele" scarves, late 1960s.
Silk twill, 90 x 90 cm.

"My father started his first company in the early 1950s and the Marquis Emilio Pucci did the same. We share a story between us. The art of savoir faire, the mannequins, the high-quality fabrics, and the never-ending, constant search for beauty."

— Andrea Bonaveri

Handbag featuring the "Campanule" motif. "Bonaveri — A Fan of Pucci" exhibit, Emilio Pucci Heritage Hub in Palazzo Pucci, June 2018. Photo: Lapo Quagli.

Opposite: The hand-painted mannequins in the "Vivara" motif. "Bonaveri — A Fan of Pucci" exhibit at the Emilio Pucci Heritage Hub, June 2018. Photo: Lapo Quagli.

Pages 366/367: Main Gallery, "Bonaveri — A Fan of Pucci" exhibit, Emilio Pucci Heritage Hub in Palazzo Pucci, June 2018. Photo: Lapo Quagli.

Pages 368/369: The Art Mannequins, each representing a recurring theme of the style of Emilio Pucci. "Bonaveri — A Fan of Pucci" exhibit at the Emilio Pucci Heritage Hub, June 2018. Photo: Lapo Quagli.

Imagining the Universe

When it comes to Pucci, "jet set" has so many meanings it is like an onion: peel off one layer and another reveals itself. Its roots are, as always, in the history of Emilio Pucci himself, who was both a pilot who understood the power of fast planes from an early age, and a social superstar, spending time in the company of a coterie of celebrities that encompassed everyone from Paloma Picasso to Sophia Loren and Gloria Guinness. Later he dressed a different kind of jet set, becoming the first fashion designer to create uniforms for airlines—Braniff in 1965 and Quantas in 1974, when the glamor of airplane travel was still at its height—thus developing a cross-industry synergistic marketing tool that other designers continue to exploit. Perhaps the ultimate expression of his interest, however, came when Pucci was asked to design the logo for the Apollo 15 space mission in 1971, which he created out of three bird-like flying forms, and which gave him yet another world to imagine and draw. Curvilinear lines of lime, fuchsia, and blue? Spiraling swirls of purple and cream? Nothing less than comets and stars. What looks abstract is actually a piece of the puzzle, and from aeronautics to fabric development, it all comes down to technology and innovation—then and now.

Lieutenant Emilio Pucci on an Italian Air Force Torpedo bomber, 1942.

Pages 372/373: Detail of "Anonimo" drawing for a scarf, 1960s. Pen, whitening fluid, and crayon on photocopy, 93 x 90 cm.

"He understood the airline uniform and the space shuttle—he came from uniforms. He was in the air force. It was part of his own experience."
— Anna Piaggi

"Aeronautica" scarf.
Silk twill, 90 x 90 cm.

Opposite: Lieutenant Emilio Pucci, pilot of the 204th squadron of Torpedo bombers of the Italian Air Force, 1942.

585

"Aquila" scarf, 1979.
Silk twill, 90 x 90 cm.

Opposite: Lieutenant Emilio Pucci at the Derna base, Rhodes, with one of the fighter planes, 1942.

"Pianeti" scarf, 1970s.
Silk twill, 90 x 90 cm.

Opposite: Detail of "Cometa" scarf, 1970. Silk twill, 90 x 90 cm.

Opposite: "Viva" trousers in Emilioform, with matching shoes and printed silk twill shirt, in the "Calcio in Costume" motif. Spring/Summer 1961 Collection.

Uniform for Braniff International: overcoat in reversible double wool and pink- or plum-colored mini dress, with matching leggings, scarf, and shoes, 1968.

THE GARRETT COR
AIR CRUISERS DI
BELMAR, N.J.

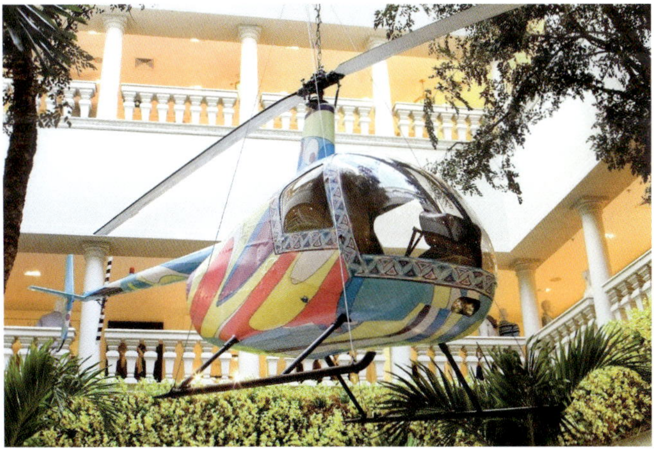

Opposite: The evening version of the Capsule in Emilioform, embroidered with small corals, and the daywear version, in black and white. Spring/Summer 1961 Collection.

Above: "Marmo" scarf, 1968. Silk twill, 90 x 90 cm.

Left: Helicopter decorated with the "Lavalamp" motif. Daslu Store, São Paulo, Brazil, 2006.

Uniforms for the hostesses of Braniff International Airways, 1971: two dresses in pale pink Qiana with prints in tones of pink; one high-waisted dress, medium-length skirt, short sleeves, and ruffled neckline; the other with square neckline, knee-length skirt, short sleeves, and low waist. Each of the dresses can be worn with or without Qiana trousers in matching print. Umbrella, shoulder-strap bag, scarf; raspberry-pink shoes by Baldino. Photos: Braniff International Dallas.

Uniforms for Braniff International, 1965/71. From the left: suit with jacket and skirt, with "Bolla" bucket hat and matching boots, 1965; printed polyester jersey dress, with matching "Derby" leggings and hat, 1966; pink- or plum-colored mini dress with matching leggings, scarf, and shoes, 1968; Qiana dress in pale pink or printed in tones of red, pink, and plum and three tones of green, high-waisted, knee-length skirt, short sleeves, and ruffled neckline, matching pink trousers, umbrella and shoes, 1971.

"Braniff" scarf.
Cotton gabardine, 90 x 90 cm.

Opposite: A life-size model of the Lockheed supersonic airplane is the background for the Braniff Airways hostesses, wearing uniforms created by Emilio Pucci in 1966: printed polyester jersey mini dresses and leggings in pale blue or pink, transparent raincoat and "Bolla" helmet to be worn over the "Derby" hat. Matching shoes in pink or turquoise leather by Baldino.

NO STEP

8

"It was the first brand to make little jersey slip dresses you could stick in your bag and get on a plane. There was such glamor to that idea of seeing the world, but it was a natural outgrowth from his life and social set."

— Holly Brubach

Opposite: Hostesses in Pucci uniforms on a BI tractor. The four basic looks: wool and acrylic overcoat with the "space" helmet, two-colored dress, skirt suit, and jersey top with puff trousers.

Hostess "Bubble" space helmet.
Photos © Braniff Collection, History of Aviation Collection, Special Collections Department, McDermott Library, The University of Texas at Dallas.

Sequence from the video "The Air Strip," produced to highlight the versatility and comfort of the Braniff uniforms designed by Pucci. From the overcoat to the "space" helmet, from the skirt suit or the dress to the jersey top with puff trousers; all in the seven new colors of the Braniff aircraft. Photo © Peter Gössel.

Hostess with pink dress and orange coat. Photo © Braniff Collection, History of Aviation Collection, Special Collections Department, McDermott Library, The University of Texas at Dallas.

Opposite: Uniforms for Braniff hostesses, 1971: Qiana printed dress with the "Braniff" motif, with high-waisted, knee-length skirt, short sleeves, and ruffled neckline, the dress can be worn with or without trousers. Other accessories featuring the same motif are: umbrella, shoulder bag, scarf, and Pucci by Baldino shoes. Photo: Lorenzo del Turco.

Old and new Braniff hostess uniforms through the ages. The bright colored uniforms are designed by Emilio Pucci. Photos © Braniff Collection, History of Aviation Collection, Special Collections Department, McDermott Library, The University of Texas at Dallas.

Opposite: Orange leather boot for the Braniff hostesses' uniforms, Emilio Pucci by Baldino.

Above and opposite: Uniforms for the hostesses of the Italian Pavilion at the World Expo in Osaka, 1972. Printed silk jersey "Vivara" mini dress in different color tones, with matching turban, handbag, and shoes.
Photos: Publifoto.

PAN AM

"The Marchese had been one of the main innovators on the fashion scene in the second half of the 20th century: he broke with the codes of the preceding fashions by introducing technology, casualness, easiness, lightweight travel, strong colors and recognizable prints. No one had done that before."

— Christian Lacroix

Uniforms for the hostesses of the Italian Pavilion at the World Exposition in Osaka. Gold vinyl coat, boots, and hat; matching leggings and handbag, in the "Vivara" motif. Fall/Winter 1972 Collection. Photo: Publifoto.

AN AMERICAN
50

Outfit with gold lurex mini dress and overcoat; matching shoes. Spring/ Summer 1967 Collection.

Opposite: Cocktail outfit with silver vinyl mini skirt worn over silver lamé top and pendant earrings. Fall/Winter 1966 Collection. Photo: Lumachi.

"He was very focused on macro issues, like aesthetics, but also micro issues, like technical aspects of the products. I remember deep and elaborate studies we did together, both about the width of the fabric —we moved from 90/95 centimeters to 134/145— and about the change of the count—the thickness of the silk yarn, since in China it was impossible to find silk at 13/15 and so we had to use 20/22, without changing the quality of the final product."

— Mario Boselli

Opposite: Gold vinyl raincoat, matching dress, boots, and bucket hat. Fall/Winter 1967 Collection. Photo: Ernst Zijnen.

Top: "Top of the World" evening palazzo pajamas with long flared trouser-skirt in gold brocade. Spring/Summer 1966 Collection. Photo: Lumachi.

Bottom: Evening "Chiardiluna" palazzo pajamas in gold and silver vinyl, sandals. Spring/Summer 1966 Collection. Photo: Lumachi.

Top: The medal given to Laudomia by her father. It is one of nine medals given by NASA to Emilio Pucci in recognition for his work on the logo. The medals were taken to the Moon by the astronauts of the space mission, and then brought back to Earth. Courtesy of Laudomia Pucci.

Above: Emilio Pucci with the logo he designed for the Apollo 15 NASA mission, 1971. Photo: Lumachi.

Opposite: Emilio Pucci visiting NASA Space Center, in front of a model of the lunar excursion module in Houston, Texas, September 30, 1969. Photo: NASA.

"Stella" scarf, 1970s.
Silk twill, 90 x 90 cm.

Opposite: Embroidered down jacket. Fall/Winter 2018/19 Collection. Model: Elina V. Stylist: Maria Giulia Riva. *Gioia*, September 2018. Photo © Domingo Nardulli/ doubleone_studio.

"Mac 2" scarf, 1967.
Silk twill, 90 x 90 cm.

"Satellite" scarf, 1968.
Silk crêpe, 90 x 90 cm.

Top: Silk crêpe evening dress in the "Sole" scarf motif. Spring/Summer 2007 Collection. *Vogue* Australia, 2005. Photo © Blaise Reutersward.

Bottom: Emilio Pucci, sketch for "Sole" drawing, 1970s. Pencil and pen on paper, 13 x 13 cm.

Opposite: Drawing for the "Sole" scarf, 1970s. Crayon on paper, 100 x 90 cm.

"Pucci embodied everything that was new when he began, and the brand never lost anything of his modernity. It was the fruit of an ever-successful alchemy: on one side, the roots of ancestral tradition without obsolete or sterile immobility and on the other, of an equal level and strength, the taste for innovation, research, the proximity with science, technology, and art. It's not for nothing that the image that remains is this dandy Prince in Florentine armor who works with NASA without forgetting his own intoxicating sense of color."

— Christian Lacroix

Pucci Galaxy

Because of the idea that informed the creation, Pucci always described a world; there was no limit to where the brand could go, as long as the journey demanded a sense of freedom, of possibility, and of joy. And because Emilio Pucci had been in the business of smashing expectations since he opened his shop in 1949, the mere fact that at the time fashion designers, in their ivory towers as opposed to their beach resorts, did not make towels or face cloths, was simply another opportunity for amusement. If Pucci saw his job as answering a need, then there was also a need for accessories, and home furnishings, and scent, and he would fill it. So what began with solving the sartorial problems posed by skiing, swimming, and travel, soon expanded to encompass the creation of tights and hats and handkerchiefs, bags and gloves and boots. There were the traditional extensions—perfumes (Vivara, first introduced in 1965 and re-released for the 60th anniversary) and lingerie—and the nontraditional ones: cars (a Lincoln Continental, in 1977), a Vespa, china (with Rosenthal), rugs and then furniture, courtesy of Cappellini, which engineered collaborations with renowned designers Patrick Norguet and Piero Lissoni, in 2001 and 2002 respectively, producing an iconic series of chairs and sofas that is still available today. And then, more recently, the prestigious mosaics decoration line with Bisazza (2014), espresso cups with illy (2015), a new childrenswear line (2017), customized mannequins in Emilio Pucci fabrics with Bonaveri (2018), a hospitality project with Rocco Forte Hotel Savoy in Florence (2018), a sustainable stainless-steel bottle with 24 Bottles (2019). For the mentality that propelled the expansion then and now is the same: object and design must be powered by identical drivers, and only then will there be legitimacy in the partnership. Case in point: a 2004 60-foot sloop built by Wally Yachts, designed, from sail to banquette, by Pucci, and inspired by ... the yacht Emilio himself used to own. As Alice Bingham Gorman, an ex–Pucci model, recalled in a *Vogue* memoir of her time with the Marchese, "he said, 'designing clothes for women is natural for me. But, of course, I design other things as well—I always talk about designing automobiles with my friend Gianni Agnelli.'" As with everything Pucci, the impetus is not theoretical, but emotional and practical.

Page 412: Printed silk jersey top with "Oroscopo" scarf motif, printed Lycra leggings with "Portici" panel motif. Spring/Summer 1990 Collection.

Pages 414/415: "Cappelli di Paglia" drawing, 1952/53. Tempera and china ink on paper, 135 x 140 cm.

Anna Piaggi with a Pucci coat in the "Love" motif and a Pucci Collectible bag, during the reception in Villa di Granaiolo for the launch of the new "Vivara" perfume, May 2007.

Opposite: Jennifer Lopez wears a printed silk chiffon caftan in the "Wings" motif. Spring/Summer 2006 Collection. *Hello Magazine*, February 2007. Photo © Richard Mclaren. Courtesy Emilio Pucci Archive, Florence.

Opposite: Alicia Keys wearing vintage Pucci dress and scarf at the 2019 Grammys. Photo © Jeff Kravitz/Getty Images.

Madonna wearing a printed silk jersey T-shirt in "Magnolia" scarf motif, 1990. *Panorama*, Spain, 1990.
Photo © Juan José Gonzalez.

Beyoncé wearing a custom Emilio Pucci beaded dress and boots, "The Mrs. Carter Show World Tour," New York, 2013.
Photo © Kevin Mazur/Getty Images.

Opposite: Kate Moss in a vintage printed silk jersey dress.
Photo © Juergen Teller.

Pages 422/423: The 60th anniversary of the Pucci Company, May 19, 2007. Installation by Gerard Cholot in the courtyard of Palazzo Pucci.
Photo: Alessandro Ciampi.

LE BOOK PARIS 2005
LE BOOK PARIS 2005
LE BOOK PARIS 2005
EMILIO PUCCI

PHOTOGRAPHIE
ART DIRECTION
PARIS
2005
BOOK

CHILI DOGS
PINK'S
SINCE 1939
Grads
Dads

MADE SPECIAL FOR
PINK'S
DOGS

Pages 424/425: Special project "Le Book"; the model wears a printed silk jersey dress with the "Fantasia" motif, 2004. *ID*, December/January 2004/05. Photo Fernando Etulain © Le Book.

Pages 426/427: Pucci Barbie, wearing printed top and trousers. *Barbie Loves L.A.*, June 2003. Photo © Greg LaVoi.

Miniature display showing the "Collectible Collections," 2007/09. Collectible Collections are a reissue of historic Emilio Pucci dresses and accessories.

"I believe we are in a revolutionary period. That is, evolution is moving so fast that it's revolution. And in such periods I believe there are people who are the channels through which it passes. I feel, in my way, I am one of those channels."

— Emilio Pucci

Top: Leather handbag with knit "turtle-neck" opening. Fall/Winter 1953 Collection.

Bottom: Bucket handbag with knit "turtle-neck" closure. Fall/Winter 1953 Collection.

Opposite: Christy Turlington wears a printed silk jersey top and matching leggings in the "Fiori di campo" motif, small velvet bag in the "Astro" motif. Fall/Winter 1990/91 Collection. Photo © Patrick Demarchelier/Condé Nast *Vogue* Italia November 1990.

Handbag with woven straw basket, bamboo handle, and printed silk twill scarf in the "Porticato" motif, 1964. 43 x 45 cm.

Sketches for handbags, late 1950s. China ink on paper, 26 x 30 cm.

Below left: Small box purse in printed cotton velveteen in the "Rio" motif, 1967. 13 x 13 cm.

Below right: Printed cotton gabardine clutch handbag in the "Rio" motif, 1967. 21 x 17 cm.

"I have many Pucci shirts, but I think my favorite pieces are the handkerchiefs. I put them in my handbags, and they just cheer me up every time I open the bag."

— Marina Rust

Handbag with double envelope closure on the front, in silk twill scarf borders in the "Vivara" motif, 1970s. 19 x 22 cm.

Opposite: Sketch of an evening handbag by Erlikh, Fall/Winter 2004/2005 Collection. *Marie Claire* France, February 2005.
Illustration © Eduard Erlikh.

ERlikH

Cotton velvet handbag with "Ventaglio" motif, 1960s. 17 x 20 cm.

Small box handbag in printed silk twill in the "Fiocchetti" motif (1966) with golden metal handle. "Collectible Collection" (reissue) 2007. 12 x 20 cm.

Cotton velvet handbag with double envelope front closure and borders in the "Vivara" motif, 1960s. 17 x 23 cm.

Box purse in printed silk crêpe with the "Bersaglio" motif; gold metal ring handle, 1977. 19 x 14 cm.

Sketches for Emilio Pucci, Spring/Summer 2003 Collection by Christian Lacroix.

Opposite: Wide-brimmed black straw hat with miniature hats attached as decoration. Spring/Summer 1954 Collection. Photo: Lumachi.

Pages 442/443: Emilio Pucci fits a pagoda-shaped black straw hat. Spring/Summer 1961 Collection. Photo: Kurt Ammann.

Emilio

"He loved life, and he understood how to create joie de vivre around himself with his work."
— Hubert de Givenchy

Opposite: Printed cotton shirt and shorts, "oversize" wicker hat. Siciliana Collection, Spring/Summer 1955.

Printed cotton scarf with straw visor, cotton shirt in the "Emilio di Capri" motif and matching shorts, "Campanelli" belt. Spring/Summer 1952/53 Collection.
Photo: Gerard Herter.

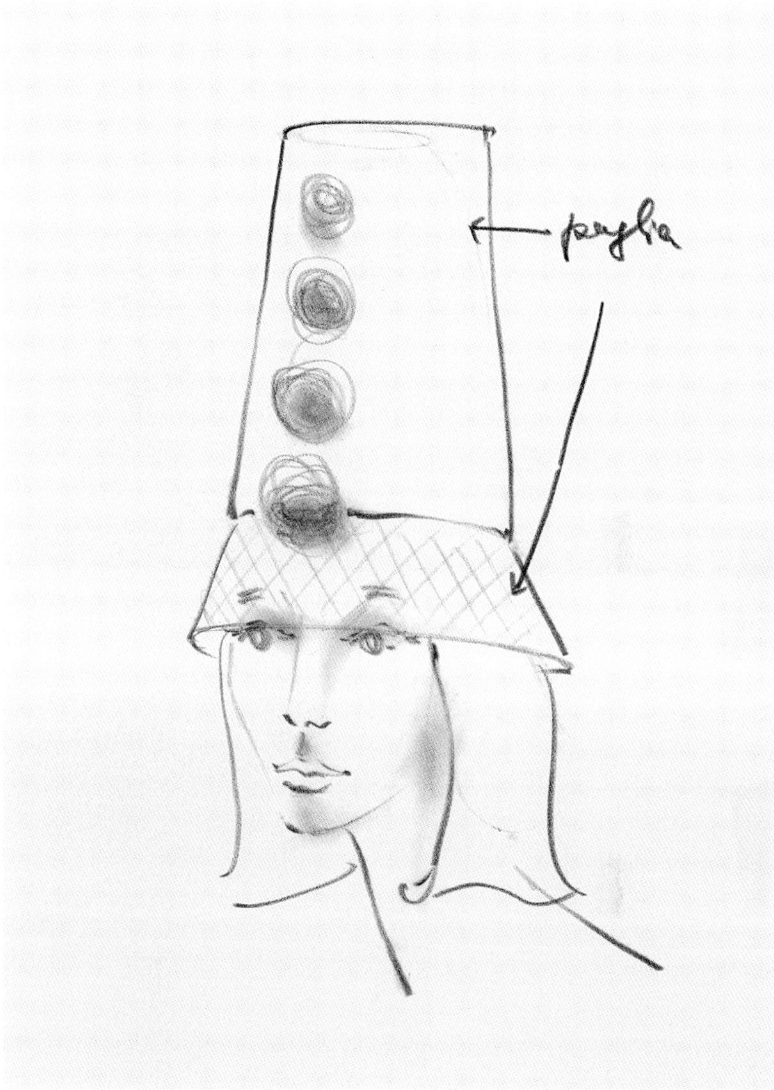

Opposite: Ivy Nicholson wears a conical straw hat over a silk twill scarf with "Isola di Capri" motif, turtleneck wool sweater with wool gabardine trousers. Fall/Winter 1952 Collection. Photo: Relang, Munich.

Sketch for a conical hat with pom-pom decorations, 1960s.

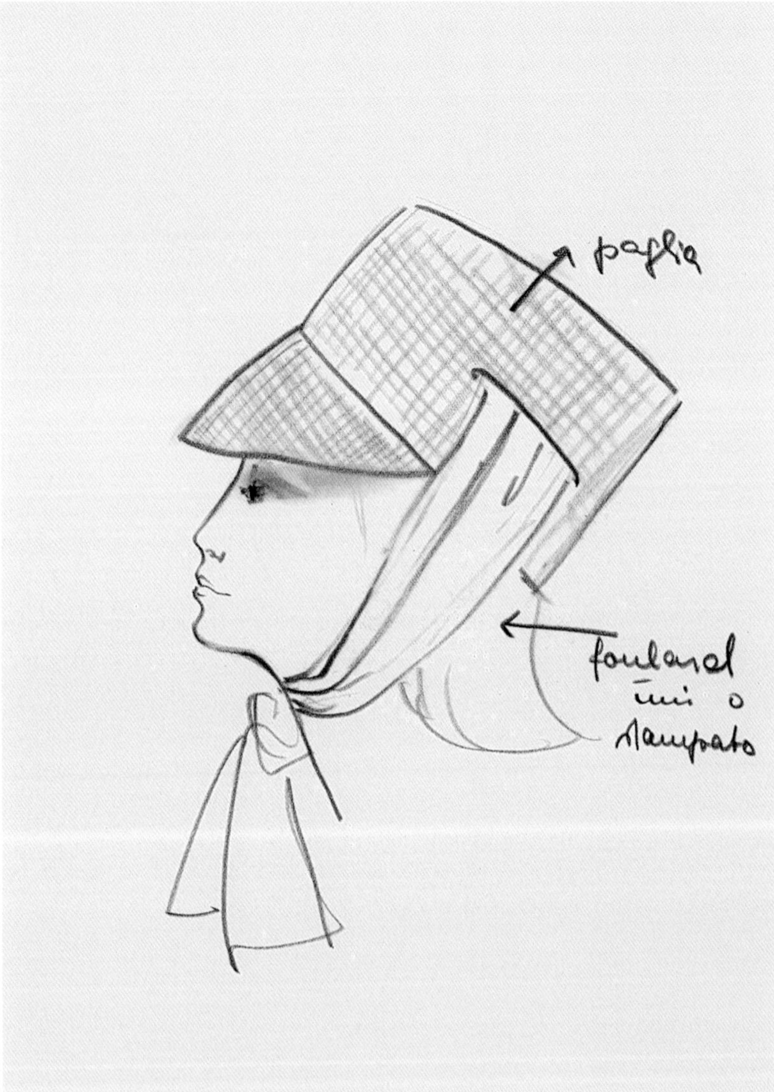

Sketch for a hat tied with a scarf, 1960s.

Opposite: Straw "Pinocchio" hat, shell necklace and top. Spring/Summer 1954 Collection.

"Mazzocchio" straw hat, worn over a silk twill scarf; silk shantung top and trousers, earrings and bracelet. Spring/Summer 1954 Collection. Model: Ivy Nicholson, Capri.

Opposite: Ivy Nicholson poses on a Capri beach with "Tagliatelle" straw hats in different colors. Spring/ Summer 1952/54 Collection.
Photos: Relang, Munich.

Silk crêpe turban with the "Vivara" motif, late 1960s.

Silk crêpe turban with the "Minareti" motif, late 1960s.

Hat with purple wool gabardine crown
and pink wool gabardine visor, 1969.

Helmet-shaped hat with visor and chin-strap in printed cotton terrycloth, 1967.

"Zuccottino" multicolored straw hat, early 1950s.

Cylindrical hat with flat crown in silk crêpe in the "Trifoglio" motif and fringes, 1970.

Philip Treacy for Emilio Pucci straw pagoda hat with long silk chiffon scarf, inspired by a late 1950s vintage Pucci hat. Spring/Summer 2005 Collection.

Printed cotton popeline scarf with small disk in colored straw decorated with cotton ruches.

Philip Treacy creation for Emilio Pucci: tall fur hat, in colored mink. Fall/Winter 2004/05 Collection.

Philip Treacy creation for Emilio Pucci:
small toque in mink with large feather.
Fall/Winter 2004/05 Collection.

Philip Treacy creation for Emilio Pucci: printed silk in the "Stella" motif, decorated with colored feathers and marabou. Spring/Summer 2004 Collection.

Philip Treacy creation for Emilio Pucci: printed silk in the "Stella" motif. Spring/Summer 2004 Collection.

Philip Treacy creation for Emilio Pucci, in the "Stella" motif decorated with colored feathers and marabou. Spring/Summer 2004 Collection.

Philip Treacy creation for Emilio Pucci:
printed silk in the "Stella" motif.
Spring/Summer 2004 Collection.

Opposite: Maria Carla Boscono wears a silk jersey turtleneck dress with "Cristallo" motif and sunglasses. Fall/Winter 2008/09 Collection. Photo © Juergen Teller.

Maria Carla Boscono backstage, wearing a silk chiffon dress with the "Stella" motif, hat by Philip Treacy for Emilio Pucci. Spring/Summer 2004 Collection. *Vogue* Germany, January 2004. Photo © Sean Cunningham.

Pages 468/469: Sandals in black and pink leather with feathers and gold sculpted wedges, skirt in cotton ottoman with "Sundial" motif. Spring/Summer 2008 Collection, Palazzo Gangi, Palermo, Italy. Photo © Juergen Teller.

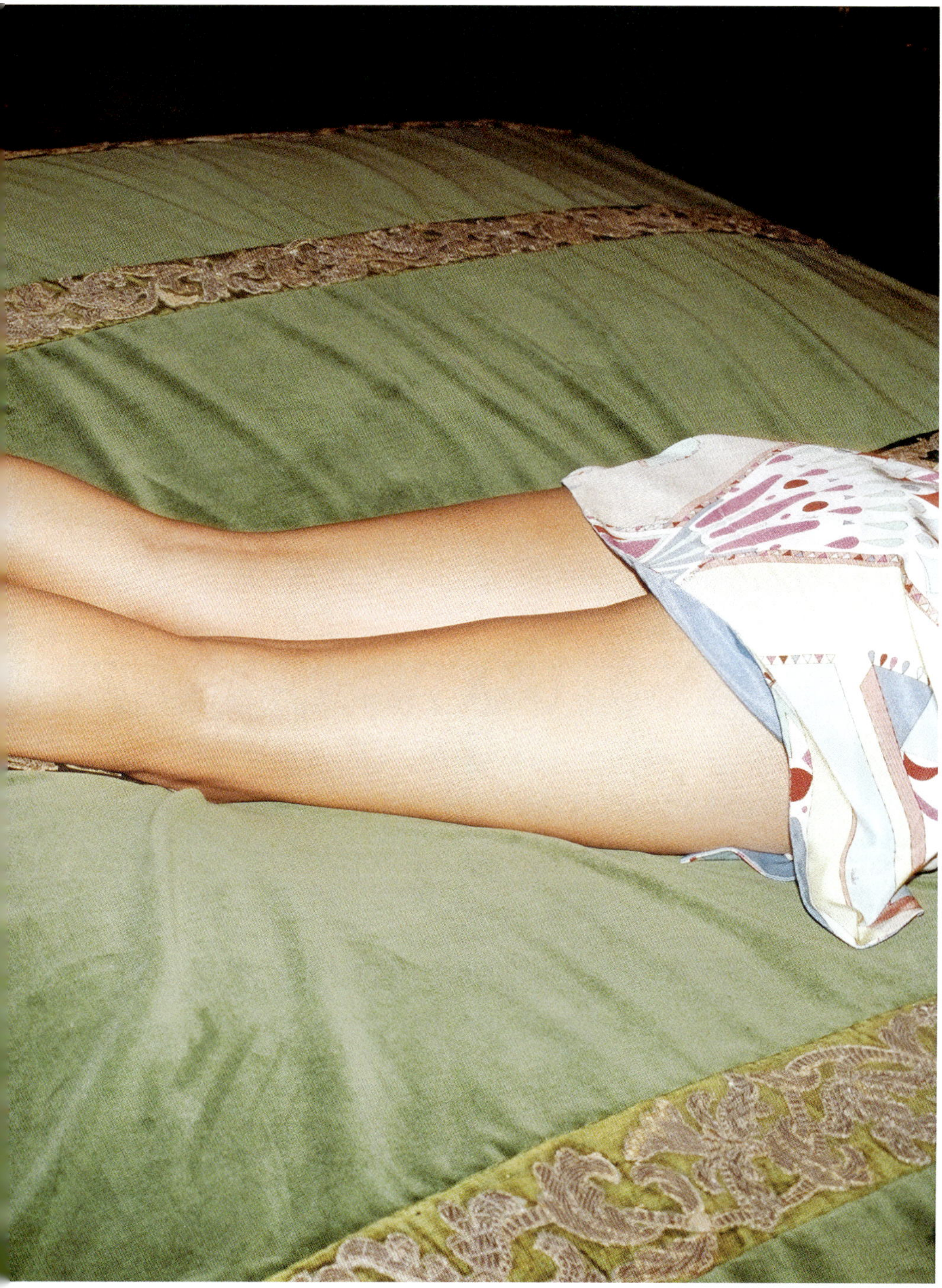

"In the 1970s I used to buy a lot of Pucci ties and handkerchiefs, and one day I was in the store on 64th and Madison, and the saleswoman there said, 'There's someone I would like you to meet'—and it was Emilio Pucci. We got to talking and I told him I had always dreamed of lining my suits in Pucci fabric, and he said that was an interesting idea, and he would do it. So from then on I would have my tailor in New York send him the fabric for my suits, and he would send back a Pucci fabric to go with it, and I would have a very conservative outside with a very surprising inside. I must have had about two or three hundred of them in the end. He was always interested in trying new things."

— Bill Koch

Black suede sandals. Fall/Winter 2004/05 Collection. *Vogue Pelle*, July 2004. Photo © Cristina Tarantola.

Opposite: Printed silk mini dress in the "Maelstorm" motif. Spring/Summer 2010 Collection. *Vogue Pelle*, January 2010. Photo © Steve Hiett/Vogue Pelle 2010.

Pages 472/473: Silk dress with "Ellisse" print and sandals with scarf laces. Spring/Summer 2003 Collection. *Vogue* Australia, April 2003. Photo © Torkil Gudnason.

VOGUE
the Glam Charts
LA FRANCE QU'ON AIME
L'atlas
Le Point
L'EXPRESS
HEUREUX ?
SCIENCE & VIE
Femme Actuelle
Astro
Une année riche en surprises
MARIONS-

Above: Crystal beads necklace by Coppola e Toppo for Emilio Pucci, ca. 1960. Courtesy of Laudomia Pucci.

Right: Sketch for buckles, 1960s. China ink on paper, 24 x 26 cm.

Opposite: Emilio Pucci with Ivy Nicholson wearing a wide boatneck silk twill cocktail dress in the "Visone" motif; necklace by Coppola e Toppo for Emilio Pucci. Spring/Summer 1955 Collection. Photo: Scrimali.

Emilio Pucci with Ivy Nicholson and Joanne Walker wearing silk twill dresses in the "Visone" motif; earrings and necklace by Coppola e Toppo for Emilio Pucci. Spring/Summer 1955 Collection. Photo: Scrimali.

Opposite top: Necklace with large cut crystal beads. Coppola e Toppo for Emilio Pucci, ca. 1960. Courtesy of Laudomia Pucci.

Opposite bottom: Drawing for a buckle, 1962. Pencil on paper, 20 x 25 cm.

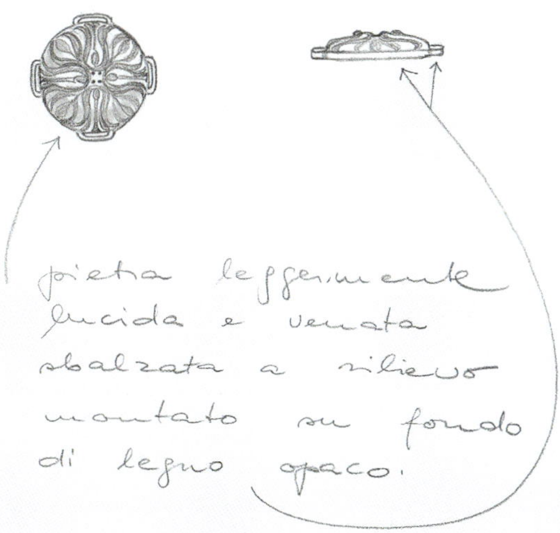
pietra leggermente
lucida e venata
sbalzata a rilievo
montato su fondo
di legno opaco.

VIVARA SUPER
Emilio Pucci

"Many people had approached me to do a makeup line, but I didn't want to do it until Guerlain, and then it was so perfect, because it wasn't just the box, but the actual colors inside that could speak to Pucci."

— Laudomia Pucci

Opposite: Advertising campaign for "Vivara" fragrance, scarf in printed silk chiffon featuring the "Vivara" motif, 1969/71. Photo: Sandro Morriconi.

Limited edition "Guerlain" scarf, 2006. Silk twill, 80 x 80 cm.

"The junior line combines the spirit of Emilio Pucci with the respect for children and their world to create clothes that are beautiful, of excellent quality, and full of the joy that is important to this brand."

— Laudomia Pucci

Advertising campaign for Emilio Pucci Junior Line for Simonetta. Fall/Winter 2018/19 Collection. Photo © Marco Tassinari/art direction Petra Barkhof.

Opposite: Advertising campaign for Emilio Pucci Junior Line for Simonetta. Spring/Summer 2018 Collection. Photo © Marco Tassinari/art direction Petra Barkhof.

Emilio
Emilio
NW
NE
E
SE
S
EMILIO
Capriccio di Capri
LUNEDI
MONDAY

Window display in Sydney: outfit with jacket and cotton shorts or trousers, matching striped top, multicolored straw hat and clogs. From the Emilio di Capri Collection, Spring/Summer 1953/54. Photo: Phil Ward Studios Pty LTD.

Opposite: Emilio Pucci autographs rugs on display at the Museo Nacional de Arte Decorativo in Buenos Aires, 1970. Photo: Sara Facio-Alicia d'Amico, Buenos Aires.

Façade of Ginza Boutique, Tokyo. Photo © Daici Ano. Courtesy Emilio Pucci Archive, Florence.

Opposite: Cappellini "Rive Droite" armchair, by Patrick Norguet, covered in leather printed in the "Lillium" motif.
Photo: Santi Caleca.

Interior of Saint Tropez boutique.
Photo: Santi Caleca.

Porcelain vases designed for Rosenthal, mid-1970s.

Porcelain vases designed for Rosenthal,
"Zadig" motif, mid-1970s.

Hand-painted terracotta vases with anthropomorphic shapes, 1953.

Right: Rosenthal porcelains, "Quadratini" motif, 1961.

Below: Emilio Pucci at the presentation of his porcelain series at the Rosenthal showroom in Düsseldorf, 1961.

Outfit with cotton T-shirt with contrasting edges, cotton gabardine shorts and hat. From the "Vespa Piaggio" Collection, Spring/Summer 1978. Vespa "Emilio Pucci," a special edition produced in 1978.

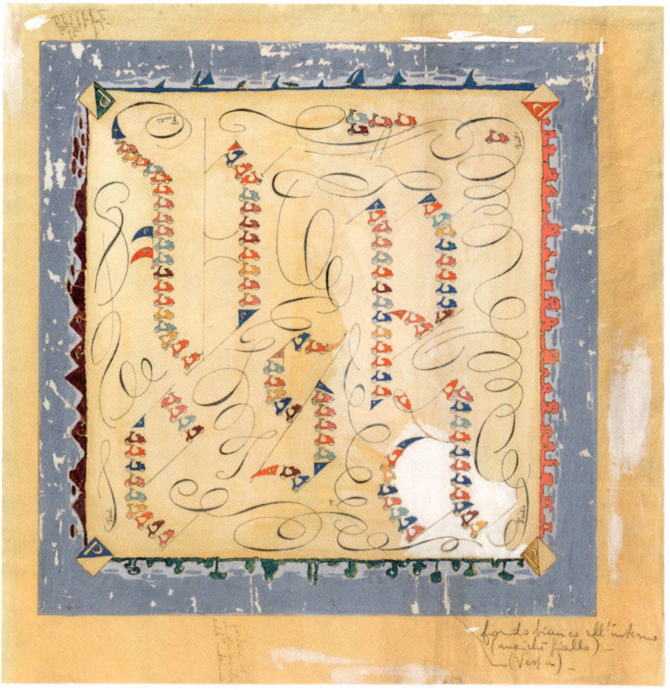

Above: "Vespa Piaggio" drawing, 1952. China and tempera on paper, 49 x 49 cm.

Left: A scooter designed by Emilio Pucci in 1947.

"At one point, we were both among a number of designers General Motors contracted to do a 'designer car': we each got to decorate a car in our favorite colors and accessories and we went together to Palm Beach and Texas for the launch. They wanted to take our picture with our cars in very special locations, and it was so hot, while we waited all our makeup started to melt. We laughed so hard."

— Hubert de Givenchy

Drawing for an advertisment for the Ford Lincoln Continental Mark IV, a limited edition Emilio Pucci for Ford Lincoln Mark VI, 1977.

Opposite: Emilio Pucci for Ford: special edition of the Lincoln Mark VI, 1981.

2833

"When I backed the women's team for the America's Cup in 1995 I asked Laudomia to design scarves as part of the team's dress uniforms. Often with boats you want a real statement as part of your spinnaker, and although I didn't think Pucci print would work on the sail, it made that impact as part of the uniform."

— Bill Koch

"A3" scarf, created for the *A3* boat; America's Cup 2003. Silk twill, 90 x 90 cm.

Opposite: *Wallyño,* the 18-meter Wally sailing yacht with Pucci-designed gennaker, 2003. Photo © Carlo Borlenghi.

"My husband loves sailing and one day we were in St. Moritz and started talking to Luca Bassani, founder of Wally Yachts, and the subject of doing a boat came up, and we thought: Why not? It wasn't for business, but for fun. I remember going to Portofino and sitting on the floor doing the signatures on the giant sail; it was more than 100 square meters. But it had a terrific impact."

— Laudomia Pucci

Exterior decoration of *Wallyño* with printed terrycloth cushions featuring the "Rio" motif, 2003.

Pages 500/501: Bisazza mosaic featuring the Emilio Pucci "Amelie" motif, 2014. Photo © Matteo Imbriani.

Pages 502–505: Emilio Pucci for illy Art Collection, 2016. Model: Lorelle Rayner. Photo © Linus Ricard

Opposite: Espresso cup featuring the "New York" motif from Cities of the World Collection.

Espresso cup featuring the historic "Battistero" motif.

"This is the first time we've ever worked with a fashion brand. But Emilio Pucci was himself an artist, and it made perfect sense to bring his enduring vision and unmistakable style to life."

— Carlo Bach

Top: Espresso cup featuring the "London" motif from Cities of the World Collection.

Bottom: Espresso cup featuring the "Avenue Montaigne" motif from Cities of the World Collection.

Opposite: Espresso cup featuring the "Piazza di Spagna" motif from Cities of the World Collection.

illy
Art Collection

SAVOY

"Envisioning this unique project with Hotel Savoy meant working closely with Olga and it's been a wonderful treat. For the very first time in hospitality and in the Emilio Pucci history, we have translated the creativity which this city inspires by merging the elegance of the Savoy with the vibrancy and sophistication that is embedded in the Pucci codes and in the city of Florence itself, adding Pucci touches in the lobby and restaurant area of the hotel."

— Laudomia Pucci

Opposite: Terrace of the Irene Restaurant at Hotel Savoy—Rocco Forte Hotels. The tables feature the "Rocco Forte" scarf representing Piazza della Repubblica in Florence, 2018. Photo: Lapo Quagli.

Wool rug featuring the "Lamborghini" motif in the lobby of the Hotel Savoy—Rocco Forte Hotels, Florence, 2018. Photo: Lapo Quagli.

Historic boutique, Emilio Pucci Heritage Hub in Palazzo Pucci, June 2018. The boutique was reimagined in its original rooms with a Pucci colors wallpaper inspired by "The Coloured Rooms" installation curated by Maria Luisa Frisa in 2007. Photo: Lapo Quagli.

"Elements" exhibition curated by Maria Luisa Frisa. The exhibition was set in Villa di Granaiolo during the LVMH—Les Journées Particulières, 2016. Photo: Lapo Quagli

The publisher wishes to thank the photographers, archives, agencies, magazines, and newspapers that granted permission to reproduce works and gave support in the making of the book. If not otherwise specified, the reproductions originated from Emilio Pucci Archive. The copyright of the works illustrated, if not indicated differently, is held by the artists, their heirs or estates, or their assignees. Despite intensive research it has not always been possible to establish copyright ownership. Where this is the case we would appreciate notification.

All the quotations published in this book are from interviews conducted by Vanessa Friedman, apart from the following. The quotations on pp. 23 and 50: *Pucci Jet-Set Revolution*, Amy Fine Collins, Vanity Fair, 2000. The quotations on pp. 25 and 41: Interview, Oriana Fallaci, *L'Europeo*, September 1963. The quotation on p. 159: @diet_prada. The quotation on p. 504: illy, Press Release, October 2016. The quotation on p. 507: Rocco Forte Hotels, Press Release, March 2018. The quotation on p. 429: *Home Furnishings Daily*, 1969.

Directed and produced by
Benedikt Taschen, Los Angeles
Design by Armando Chitolina, Milan

English translation:
Antonia Reiner, Toronto

Hohenzollernring 53, D-50672 Köln
taschen.com

Original edition:

Printed in Bosnia-Herzegovina
ISBN 978-3-7544-0020-3